Dean Koontz And The Art Of Transcendent Storytelling

Avery J. Caldwell

GLOBAL EAST-WEST. LONDON.

Copyright © 2025 by Avery J. Caldwell.

"What Do You Know About?"   A Global East-West Series.

All rights reserved. No part of this book may be reproduced in any manner whatsoever without written permission, except for brief quotations incorporated into critical articles and reviews.

Contents

1. Introduction — 1
   A Literary Icon Beyond Genre

2. The Early Years — 19
   From Humble Beginnings to Aspiring Writer

3. Themes of Darkness and Light — 39
   Influences from a Troubled Childhood

4. Crafting the Uncategorisable — 61
   The Blending of Genres

5. Whispers and Breakthroughs — 81
   Achieving Literary Success

6. The Odd Thomas Phenomenon — 101
   A Beloved Character Enters the Scene

7. Behind the Scenes   123
   Koontz's Meticulous Writing Process

8. Moral Convictions in Narrative Form   147
   Depth Beyond Thrills

9. A Man Behind the Stories   167
   His Personal Life and Inspirations

10. Legacy and Influence   185
    Transcending Boundaries in Popular Fiction

Bibliographic Selection   205

I
Introduction

A Literary Icon Beyond Genre

Contextualising an Enigmatic Legacy

Considering the factors that have shaped a lasting impact on the world of literature, it appears that not many can match the mystic legacy of this literary figure. The author's body of work is marked by an astonishing and distinctive voice that cuts across the fabric of literary genres and their rigid delineations. There is a remarkable sense of originality, depth, and innovation that characterises all of his writings, from the early ones to the latest published works, which distinguishes him from his contemporaries. This distinguished reputation has, in the words of writers, not only won praise but also captivated a multitude of readers around the globe. The author's unabashed ability to combine suspense, mystery, horror, and philosophical discourse into a single narrative showcases an unparalleled genius. In addition to that, the clear and unapologetic treatment of moral issues, human nature, and existence, while mercilessly torn apart by literature, speaks profoundly of the author's attempt to test the limits of literature.

The influence of his work on modern literature marks one of the many ways this public figure continues to be relevant today, and understanding his legacy requires a grasp of this fact. His literary work... both inspires and resonates with veteran enthusiasts and new readers alike, reflecting his boundless legacy. He provided richly thoughtful ideas to consider and deep insights to draw from in each and every one of his profound and well-crafted narratives, showcasing an unmatched ability of literary craftsmanship. Striking a balance between the strange and the profound... this chapter aims to exemplify the unique range of contributions the author has made that establish him not only as a literary icon but a perpetual monument in the world of letters too.

A Unique Voice Among Peers

Dean Koontz is a contemporary author whose distinguished literary accomplishments transcend a specific genre. He has earned distinction for the rare combination of suspense, horror, science fiction, and the supernatural, creating a voice for himself in a plethora of works. However, unlike many of his contemporaries, Koontz does not limit himself to a single genre or theme; he prefers to explore untouched terrains where complex emotions are skillfully handled. This has won him widespread readership, and garnered respect from critics and writers alike.

One can argue that the most prominent feature of Koontz's novels is his narrative detail, which helps construct engrossing new worlds that immediately capture the reader's attention. He possesses the rare skill of blending heart-wrenching emotion with bone-chilling suspense. By combining psychological insight with strange metaphysical elements, Koontz successfully brings richness and depth to his stories, ensuring audiences are not just engaged, but fully immersed in his narratives.

Koontz's expressive prose and storytelling prowess mark him as one of the distinguished authors. All of his compelling novels with well-defined characters and intricately filled plots demonstrate a commitment to excellence that defines him as a consummate professional. It is easy to observe that Koontz does not restrict his work to the boundaries of a single genre. His eclectic body of work is a testament to his pursuit of broadening the limits of narrative construction which makes him a true original and innovator in the world of literature. His storytelling prowess is something to be admired and respected.

Navigating the Literary Landscapes

The odyssey of Koontz as an author has been intricately woven with the curvilinear, ever-shifting realities of literature. Within this terrain, he has carved a niche for himself, boldly transcending convention to pummel readers into submission with a plethora of storytelling. As he moves through a maze of creation and original ideas, Koontz combines an element of suspense and horror with scientific and philosophical critique and all themes under the sun – signifying a ginormous leap within the world of sophisticated contemporary fiction.

Through different fields of literature, one may note that Koontz has traversed the waters, including the facets of the human psyche, exploring extremes of morality, existentialism, and the peculiarities of the human condition. Within these multi-layered domains, he welcomes his audience towards an intelligent completion of a passage ill-posed within the conventional boundaries of storytelling. In doing this, Koontz acknowledges fiction as a transcendent masterwork of emotions and thoughts in which people are bound within a profound connection through the words, which, unlike the passing of time, is timeless.

While coming closer to reality, it is remarkable how vivid the imagination of Koontz appears to be, for his ability to tell tales capturing both the heart and the mind is beyond this world. As he ventures towards alien spheres of literature, he encounters his readers with a paradox of extreme recognition and strange illusions that erode the fine boundaries between perception and thought. Bestowing his readers with the transforming odyssey, which is encompassed with his enchanting prose and the thrilling fables of his characters, Koontz not only earns the title of a literary explorer but also a literary magician with unlimited outbursts of creativity.

Pushing the boundaries of storytelling and challenging preconceptions takes center stage in Koontz's deft navigation of literary landscapes. The unexplored frontiers of his literary expression serve as avenues to unearth profound truths and existential revelations that resonate deeply with readers. To hearken back to his boundless spirit as an explorer of narrative realms, he not only inflames the imagination but inspires awe and wonder in readers as they embark on a thrilling journey for self-reflection. Through his adept maneuvering of the myriad terrains of literature, Koontz continues to sculpt the essence of storytelling to mark a legacy that defies expectations and attests to the transformative magic of fiction.

Breaking Conventional Barriers

Throughout his career, Dean Koontz has defied conventional practices, which has made him one of the first to practice cross-genre writing. Overstepping the traditional boundaries, Koontz does not shy away from integrating horror, suspense, mystery, science fiction, and the supernatural into a singular narrative. This approach alone has broadened his readership and challenged the very foundations of literary classification. Rather than selectively picking a genre in which to base his stories off of, Koontz puts no limitations on himself, which gives him the freedom to reinvent storytelling. His ability to traverse multiple genres with a depth of skill and artistry allows his works to transcend rigid genre categorizations and inject a wide spectrum of emotions, themes, and character development into each narrative. In accomplishing such feats, readers are given the opportunity to experience a world where concepts like reality, boundaries, and constraints are endless. Through such practices, Koontz has changed the fundamentals of writing stories and turned the attention of readers from all over the world towards him, marking a significant milestone in the realms of literature. His ability to challenge genre norms is not just intriguing, but also inspiring.

Moving past the constraints of formulaic genres, Koontz's narrative style's flexibility captures life's multifaceted and often unpredictable nature. This fulfills audiences' needs by providing stories in complex ways that transcend their differences. Such unwavering dedication toward originality and freedom in artistic expression is an enduring mark of Koontz's influence. It is also a beckoning for veteran and novice writers to rethink their creative approach. The more we explore his work, the more it is clear that breaking the so-called 'rules' is not merely a trait of Koontz's writing but an intrinsic principle that fuels the backbone of his storytelling.

Impact on Modern Literature

Dean Koontz has made an indelible mark on modern literature. He has influenced countless writers to go beyond narrative and thematic boundaries by defying traditional genre confinements. His remarkable capacity to integrate suspense, horror, science fiction, and even philosophy has transformed readers' expectations and redefined the scope of fiction. His impact is not just limited to writing; 'literary merit' is a phrase that no longer bears the same meaning after Koontz.

Through his attempt to broaden the understanding of speculative fiction's capacity for deep and profound storytelling, he was able to pierce the boundaries set by genre conventions. He is one of the very few writers who pay attention to moral dilemmas and character construction in psychology, improving the overall standard of popular fiction. This change greatly impacted the reality that readers and critics were shocked by the existence of intellectually serious documents disguised as texts in numerous genres. Koontz has, in a way, bridged the gap between modern entertainment and literary traditions, appealing to people of all ages while remaining deeply thoughtful.

His contributions have had a widening range of influences in the world of blurring literature, where lines are ever more crossed, and the combination becomes a prized feature. In other words, part of understanding his influence lies in the fact that he is not only in the business of getting people interested in modern literature; in fact, his impact serves as an indication of the strength and importance of storytelling that, even after the time and ideology have changed, continues to touch and stir the minds of many writers and readers in the ages to come.

Cross-Genre Mastery and Variance

Dean Koontz excels at almost every genre when considering the range of literature he has written. Even within his best-selling novels, primarily horror, suspense, mystery, and sometimes science fiction, he can blend in various genres so masterfully that it not only leaves the reader entertained but also surprised by the versatility of storytelling. Koontz's works are exemplary mashes of unrelated components, pulling together stories that defy singular genre pigeonholing. His works highlight his blending nimbleness thoroughly, for they contain the supernatural, psychological, and even philosophical.

Koontz does not shy away from traversing between terrifying human nature and horrific depictions with impressive narrative control, sustaining adequate thematic intricacy and unity devoid of inconsistencies. This adaptability in cross-genre writing reverberates a certain freedom from literary classification bolt in his storytelling prowess. Diverse genre explorations enrich Koontz's narratives with complexity that captivates numerous readers, a feat not many authors can achieve or aspire towards due to the varying tastes of audiences and readers alike. Koontz becomes an icon of literature for novice writers endeavouring to blend genres, proving that bounds and limits in creativity do not exist.

Because of Dean Koontz's innovative approach to genre, he is regarded as a formidable name who continues to influence the currents of contemporary literature.

An Overview of Notable Works

The modern literary scene features the works of Dean Koontz. Koontz is best known for his contributions to fiction. At the same time, he has a tremendous collection of works. His works have made an impact on the cultural landscape. Koontz had a successful career and is still considered one of the most beloved authors. He has written books across various genres – all appealing to readers worldwide. He accomplished all of this as a storyteller, a title he rightfully earned over the years. No matter the genre, he can write from heart-stopping thrillers to enlightening reflections on society. Koontz has proven to possess an exceptional level of devotion to storytelling.

Strangers is another important part of his legacy. It is an intense unraveling of the encapsulated mysteries of the mind, interlaced with an engaging plot. Watchers is a spellbinding narrative about loyalty and friendship in the unpredictable hands of fate. Intensity is perhaps his most famous work. As subdued as the title might seem, it is an unrelenting journey through the bleakest depths of humanity. Koontz can masterfully transform seemingly mundane topics into a rich blend of suspense, insight, and emotion. For this, he is praised worldwide. It is what has made him a Mark Twain Award-winning author.

Odd Thomas, which supports the supernatural and introspective themes utilising the titular character's journey, is among Koontz's most celebrated titles. Moreover, 'Lightning,' a captivating drug store and love story coupled with a time-traveling destiny, is yet further proof of his unparalleled ability to craft books that appeal to people of all ages and even transcend the boundaries of genre. Each of his works demonstrates Koontz's unique ability to tell stories that immerse readers into a captivating experience beyond genre barriers. He continues to astound and charm readers worldwide with his most notable works that combine suspense, horror, science fiction, and the study of the human condition, thus earning him the title of the literary legend.

Reception by Critics and Audience

Dean Koontz's work has received a mix of praise and criticism from the public and critics alike. Interweaving suspense alongside horror and intricate elements of human nature, Koontz has managed to capture audiences' attention spanning multiple generations, ensuring universal appeal. As noted throughout his literary career, Koontz has always been regarded as a talented storyteller, earning accolades for developing his characters and the plots within his works. Throughout the years, his storytelling abilities have captured the hearts of readers worldwide, cementing his status as a global bestselling author.

Like many successful authors, Koontz's work has not been immune to criticism. His distinctive blend of genres, which often falls outside traditional novel classifications, has sparked debates about the balance between commercialism and artistry in fiction. While some critics argue that his work is too commercial and lacks artistic depth, others appreciate the unique storytelling approach he brings to each genre.

Dean Koontz's work has a universal appeal that transcends genre boundaries. His books consistently appear on bestseller lists, indicating their popularity among a wide range of readers. Whether they are casual readers or die-hard fans, people appreciate the depth and philosophy present in Koontz's works. His narratives, combined with the strong suspense in his plots, have earned him a diverse and dedicated fan base.

It is no surprise that Koontz's portrayal of hope and resilience touches deeply with his audience. The way he explores the themes of human strength and the ability to overcome difficulties has earned him very high praise, and he shows how he moves beyond the boundaries of genres to give messages that are important to all, which is remarkable.

Koontz did not only limit his work to literature. His unique approach to telling stories has increased the adaptation of his work to other forms of media, such as film or television, increasing his influence. While they have a right to criticism, these pieces have sustained his themes and vision for society.

From the very beginning, the reception of Dean Koontz's works has been, and still is, multifaceted. His narrative style constitutes a remarkable mix of contemporary debates in literature, intertwining the author, the text, the readers, and the critics. As the subsequent chapters will demonstrate, the study of his works transcends the bounds of examination in an approach that reveals the convergence of creativity and timelessness in literature.

Core Themes and Recurrent Motifs

The contemplation of an author's core themes and motifs is an integral part of literary analysis and offers a glimpse into the architecture of the text. This is no different for Dean Koontz, whose work offers a plethora of themes and motifs that characterise his storytelling. A central focus of his narrative is the juxtaposition of light and darkness and the opposing sides of human emotion, such as love and fear. These opposites serve to make his works more profound and reflective of life. Through his characters, Koontz could analyse the human capacity to endure hardship, the power of empathy, and the possibility of redemption within chaos. It is not uncommon for his works to be thoughtful reflections of the victory of good over evil.

Setting the Stage for Deeper Exploration

In studying Dean Koontz's works, it is apparent and fascinating how various core themes and recurring motifs are woven together to form a narrative universe marked by depth and richness. These themes serve not only as a metaphoric backbone to the structure of his works but also provide a means for readers to engage with humanity in its multifaceted complexities. In assisting the reader to set the stage for further study, it is essential not to forget that Koontz's stories are more than instruments of amusement; they are also avenues for self-reflection, reflections on philosophy, and examining life's profound questions. Examining the intertwining themes, including unyielding darkness, the inscrutable nature of love and love's goodness, and our victory as a people above tribulations, assists in exploring human emotions and moral complexities in depth and breadth. The intricately described depths of psychology, moral conflict, and the struggle between hope and despair provide powerful engagement with the texts.

The intricate mazes of Koontz's storytelling invite the reader to face fundamental questions of existence and meaning, ethical dilemmas, and the truths that lie deep within humanity. The aspects of humanity that reveal its imperfections and simultaneously offer the opportunity for redemption and elevation surpass the traditional examination of the genre due to the complexity of Koontz's thematic concerns. Understanding these themes within the context of his vast body of work offers a powerful lens through which to understand the deeply rooted human realities, anxieties, and ambitions that echo in the human psyche and resonate with humanity. Hence, during this cognitive journey, where we traverse the vast landscape of Koontz's thematic reservoirs, let us keep in mind that we are not just readers but rather intellectual adventurers who set out to explore the unexplored emotional and philosophical opportunities that await us and the enigmatic questions surrounding what it means to be human.

2

The Early Years

From Humble Beginnings to Aspiring Writer

Formative Environment: Childhood in Small-Town America

Growing up in a close-knit small town in America shaped the author's worldview. The years during the developing stages of life are crucial, where the first gentle impressions and the tingle of new experiences during childhood are forever embedded into one's being. Encounters during strolls in the neighbourhood, accompanied by the feeling of ease and safety cultivated by the surrounding small community, provided the author with relentless inspiration. As time passed, elementary shapes of the world were put together, such as family, nature, and society, in addition to the ethos of discoveries waiting around every corner and within the considerable small-town backdrops. Most importantly, though, the sheer beauty of nature was further enhanced by the changing of seasons, which alternated from calm, sunny days to impending storms, snow, and a sea of colours—truly a sight to behold. Everything had something to offer; he just needed the right perspective and the will to go out and explore. There were so many things that deserved the title, such as beautiful and endless places filled with potential discoveries and overflowing with untamed wilderness yearning to be seen. Even in the simplicity of small-town branded life where everyone was familiar with one another, immense feelings of peace assured everyone on fishery autumn days and perhaps snowy ones.

The warmth and resilience of the community in the face of challenges instilled a steadfast optimism and an unwavering belief in the power of human spirit, themes that would resound throughout the author's storytelling journey. This reveals that the author's profound appreciation for humanity's complexities was carefully nurtured during his formative years immersed in small-town America. There, small-town essences instilled an intricate sense of creativity and empathy that would shape the author's future writings.

Family Dynamics and Early Challenges

An individual's formative years are usually profoundly impacted by primary relationships within the family context. For Koontz, his family dynamics and primary obstacles profoundly shaped his writing aspirations. Growing up in a small town in America, he had to grapple with family relationships against financial constraints. The quest for a better life and certain family factors created an atmosphere that drove him to escape into the world of literature and fiction. These obstacles became the first groundwork that Koontz would use to construct his life. Despite these challenges, the author's self-reliance in the face of family difficulties nurtured his ability to empathise and be compassionate, which permeated his literature.

Such chaotic family dynamics, along with the experiences of Koontz, provided him with an intricate understanding of the intertwining world of human emotions and relationships, which, in turn, helped him create multi-dimensional characters and compelling stories. The jagged kaleidoscope of unadulterated joy and sheer sorrow formed the family bonds that gave rise to profound and authentic storytelling. Through self-reflection, Koontz cultivated a rich sense of emotional intelligence, allowing him to encapsulate the essence of humanity in his writings to resonate on a deeper level with his audience.

These early hurdles in the family structure served as the primary stepping stone in life for Dean Koontz, motivating him to break free from those shackles for greater personal and creative fulfillment. The guidance he received during his struggles from some of his relatives was a pillar of support that nurtured his strong, unwavering aspirations of becoming a writer. The penetrating guidance from relatives during times of struggle proved to be the catalyst for nurturing his aspirations to become a writer. Conclusively, it was within this cauldron of biographical context that Koontz unveiled a stubborn resolve to chronicle his life experiences into damning prose amidst the turbulent tenderness of family life, which he wished to translate into his literary works.

Inspirational Figures: Teachers and Mentors

The role of one's teachers and mentors while growing up is paramount for any emerging writer. For Dean Koontz, these mentors also played a considerable role in his wish to write books, a deep-seated wish that reverberated in his soul since his early youth. He was fortunate that, as a young student, several guides or instructors came into his life who nurtured his capabilities. Storytellers were not just instructors or educators but also nurturers of creativity and imagination, which he carried for the rest of his life. Since he now appreciates the help he was given with different ideas and techniques of composing prose, there is no doubt that thanks to this help, he was able to develop, eventually, his particular style of writing. The strong propelling forces in his life assured him to attempt all manner of creative work in writing that life posed him with enduring uncertainties and challenges. Further, these outstanding persons also went out of their way to temporarily contact throughout long periods of time to offer an elixir fused with hope and dreams whose presence was enough to touch a deceased writer and awaken a dormant one inside him. Koontz had to reach out for everything provided for him if he was to place importance on the unifying conglomerate of words with which he crafted his literary aspirations and efforts. Subsequently, on persisting in eulogising their youthful years and remembering important aspects of storytellers who carved his thought processes and shaped them to suit the odyssey he overcame towards the reality that lay beyond in front of him turned out to be mirror windows through which vision was rendered multi-dimensional. Their guidance went past instruction and became integral to Koontz's motivation and artistic self. With such connections, a developing writer can find assurance, direction, and the audacity to explore the realms of imagination. These persons do not only inspire, encourage, and impart essential techniques; they grant Koontz the motivating elements that anchor one's faith in his call to do literature. When considering the responsibility and the role of the teachers and the mentors in Koontz's life, we realise the overwhelming importance of such people who mark the lives of young writers to inspire them and build for them a life loaded with literary possibilities.

The Spark of Creativity: First Storytelling Ventures

With the world around him, early Koontz had an uncanny way of interacting with it. He was perpetually interested, had a great knack for weaving stories, and deeply interested in everything. Koontz's imagination was always alive, resulting in several captivating tales that could carry a wondrous audience into realms of intrigue. It was through his earliest attempts at relaying tales that Koontz understood the astounding impact narratives had in captivating and enrapturing human emotion and attention, timing him for his future pursuits in literature. From spinning tales to his peers to meticulously inscribing fanciful tales in his notebooks, the young author was polishing his skills to bring captivating fiction to life. Every fictional piece he penned illustrated his staggering creativity, astonished by a lasting impression. These initial forays into storytelling served as milestones in Koontz's trajectory of evolving into the wordsmith he turned out to be, nurturing the power his tales possessed long before they were revealed to an audience, enchanting them for centuries. As he progressed in putting his thoughts into words, Koontz discovered the intricacies of developing plots and characters, which provided him tranquillity and a sense of purpose, fueling an unwavering love for the written word, his steadfast companion from then on.

The core of his earliest stories echoes throughout his work, testifying how those first moments of creativity were impactful. Every character, scene, and plot twist stems from the profound youthful imaginings that inspired Koontz to first take up storytelling. Indeed, the creativity first revealed in his younger years enriches his stories. Exploring the attempts at storytelling by Koontz during his childhood sheds light on the origins of what can only be described as a remarkable career. In these captivating stories, an aspiring author produces, we discover the beginnings of a timeless literary legacy.

Educational Pursuits: Navigating Academia

Amid developing his storytelling abilities and zeal for literature, an aspiring writer made his academic pursuits with self-motivation and grit. While working through his education, a wide range of subjects deeply integrated into the very framework of the aspiring writer's educational journey. The academic world offered a rich and supportive ecosystem for self-development, permitting him to break free from his local context and broaden his vistas.

During his schooling, he dug deep into the timeless works of literature, philosophy, and the arts, from which he derived profound lessons. Surrounded by sophisticated peers and learning mentors, he began grappling with the intricacies of narrative, plot, character, and theme, which, alongside his vibrant imagination, prepared him for the vast world of literature awaiting him beyond his classroom.

Aiming much higher than the conventional schooling system, the aspiring writer fully engaged himself in psychology, sociology, and natural sciences. This is diverging from literary studies, but it provides a deeper appreciation of the human condition that can later be effortlessly woven into his literary pieces.

Regardless of the hardships faced during the writer's life in pursuit of education, he developed the ability to continue performing academically. That is until the hardships along his journey began to foster his capability to bounce back from obstacles. The proposed frame of schooling did not solely serve him intellectually but provided him with an unshakeable belief in his capabilities to inevitably succeed and endure all hurdles. Every piece of study completed brought the writer closer to the reality of his dreams, which consisted of earning the title of a respected master of words.

Influences and Inspirations: Encounters with Literary Giants

While pursuing academic endeavours during his youth, he encountered numerous literary figures whose works greatly captivated him and shaped his nascent inclinations and budding interests. The assimilation of these revered authors and their monumental pieces marked a crucial junction in history—the possibility of storytelling life had been awakened. The works of legends such as Edgar Poe, H.P. Lovecraft, and Ray Bradbury immersed him in their world, and he began grappling with the exquisite nuances of brisk mastery that would eventually serve as the building blocks of his identity in the works he would one day publish. An incessant curiosity to learn more, imagine more, and innovate more ignited in him when he comprehended how timeless literature could express boundless thoughts and ideas through a single phrase, an expression, or a metaphor. Poe's macabre tales, elegantly etched with melancholy, revealed the boundless potential of atmospheric tension, and Lovecraft's cosmic terrors redefined the limits of fear and imagination. Bradbury's prose emanated nostalgia and wonder as it artfully profiled many aspects of human existence, untangling them piece by piece, thus underlying the mysteries of life. His creative aspirations had been injected with potent resolve and direction, all thanks to the indelible marks these towering figures had imprinted on him.

These figures did more than admire him; they served as his mentors, charting the course for his literary exploration. Additionally, their stories were much more than entertaining; they explored the depths of human consciousness and the strange folds of life. From this multifaceted body of influences, the young writer learned the principles of plot, character, and the magic of words—embracing the craft that would one day shape him in his narrative legacy. In the crucible of these encounters with literature, he realised that storytelling could be an act of compassion, empowerment, and disclosure, revealing the limitless possibilities of fiction as a vessel of fundamental truths. Hence, the impact of the encounters with these literary figures permeated his adolescence, shaping profoundly and enduringly the course of his literary journey.

Transition from Reader to Writer: Crafting Early Works

When Dean Koontz started reading the works of famous authors, the literary world ignited his imagination and kindled a certain interest within him. Koontz's narratives were remarkably influenced by the works of literary masters like Edgar Allan Poe, H.P. Lovecraft, and Ray Bradbury. These classic works, which he encountered during his childhood, motivated him to write and strive to achieve what he regarded as the utmost goal— to let his readers feel awe, fear, and exasperation all at once. Resting on the feeling brought about by the classics, Koontz began to refine his skill in crafting imaginary worlds by mixing feelings and was overjoyed by the results of his efforts.

Bearing the mantle of an aspiring novice writer, Koontz embarked on an adventure of self-exploration through writing, giving him the much-needed space for his creative juices to soar. In his self-exploration, he incorporated various topics and different approaches in his writing, enabling him to create something that provides readers with an experience like no other.

The written word encapsulated boundless opportunities for him as each stroke of his pen brought characters and scenarios to life that replicated and exaggerated human emotions. One can trace his early works to the profound engagement with light and darkness he later mastered in literature. These early works formed the heart of his later ones as he pioneered literary fulfilment.

The sculpting of his narrative footprint is a testimony to his union with classical literature and his experiences, which fostered a unique vision of life. This synthesis gave rise to an awaiting author's visionary works. Each of his works stood as proof of his evolving identity, an identity rich with past, dreams, and countless reflections captured in his writing.

This chapter of his writing journey reveals the beginnings of an unforgettable impact made by his creativity. The shift from reader to writer solidifies an enduring resolve to build worlds that haunt the reader's mind for a long time.

Lessons in Perseverance: Facing Rejection and Resilience

All hopeful writers face rejection, a painful aspect of the profession that requires them to push through with unyielding persistence. Her, we reflect on the experience of dealing with numerous rejections, accentuated by a barrage of critiques that range from dismissive to cruel. As frustrating as it is, this cycle is a fundamental phase for most writers to overcome. Rather, in most cases, failure is the most potent catalyst for success. In the long run, these setbacks build and empower a person's navigation skills when understanding the volatile publishing world. The true nature of writers' suffering when proposing their pieces is best captured by the emotional rollercoaster of a lifetime. This gives way to hope followed by utter disappointment, waiting to hear back from publishers or agents, only to face rejection repeatedly. Yet, from disappointment comes fertile ground for growth and multi-faceted character strengthening.

Writers evolve when they no longer perceive rejection as the ultimate judgment of their abilities or potential. Instead, it becomes an opportunity to improve. The chronicles of the most famous authors are full of stubbornness against all odds. It's often said that classics underwent countless rejections before enduring acceptance. Such stories remind us of the fact that literary success comes only after relentless hardships. When writers try to understand these lessons rather than give in to despair, they become more prepared for rejection. View rejection as motivation to enhance artistic expression. Withstand rejection and keep chasing ambitions—this is the essence of claiming literary success; the victory becomes far sweeter.

Honing the Craft: Experimentations in Style and Technique

With every new step into his writing career, Dean Koontz noticed the requirement to hone his skills and try out various techniques and styles. This was one of the stages of his life where he wanted to develop and elevate his storytelling to a new level and seek different horizons. His commitment to continuous improvement and experimentation is a testament to his dedication to the craft of writing.

While working on his books, developing the plot, and creating the structure, Koontz paid particular attention to all components of the book in detail, including the characters. He went beyond the limits of the ordinary and placed a huge variety of characters within the same book, all with incredibly distinct personalities.

He began fusing genres that would not normally go together, such as blending Suspense with horror and meaningful human drama. These moves were aimed at deepening the readers' interest, making them more attracted to a book that is difficult to categorise because of its uniqueness.

Koontz innovatively experimented with narrative voice and point of view, attempting to capture perspectives that would fully envelop readers in a literary experience. He made the most of first-person intimacy and omniscient scope, expertly weaving these voices into the rich tapestry of his storytelling.

Moreover, the author exploited symbolism and allegory to add layers of meaning and significance to his narratives. This exploration of deeper thematic undercurrents added a compelling richness to works that challenged readers to traverse the landscapes of the human condition.

Among these explorations lies an area where Koontz never wavered: prose. He never hesitated to tweak his writing and was always looking to experiment with the relationship between language and imagery. His ceaseless pursuit to perfect his art was simply an unquenchable desire for excellence, which fostered boundless creativity.

Through crafting the story, Koontz went from being a skilled storyteller to a master of flexibility in writing. After attempting countless experiments with style and technique, he left a profound mark on literature.

The Road to Publication: The First Steps towards a Writing Career

When Dean Koontz was trying to choose a path to a writing career, he went through many trials and experienced countless events that ultimately shaped his journey to publication. It was a period of relentless struggle and a huge desire for his beloved craft - storytelling. Koontz's first steps involved understanding how the publishing industry works - what a literary agent is, how to establish one, and what to do in the preparation stage for submission. Koontz pursued many publishers, trying to find trends in his specialisation that could bring him and his business some success. This period was characterised by realising that writing was not easy. Koontz tried to edit novellas, particularly rehearsed pieces, combining images from programmes and highlighting their dominance. Throughout this newly created project, he urgently contacted editors and readers worldwide.

It is clear that these relationships became accessible with brief, non-childish collaborations and constructive promotion toward the world's readers and market. He also understood that this excessive self-promotion and marketing somewhat confused both parties—in order to engage the reader and secure them.

Through public readings and workshops, Koontz utilised innovative strategies to showcase his talent. Through his tireless efforts, he finally gained attention from publishers who acknowledged the originality and depth of his writings. As acceptance letters began pouring in, Koontz felt fulfilled towards his literary aspirations. The unmatched excitement of witnessing his works prepared incrementally for submission underscored his ample dedication and limitless creativity. He encountered boundless scepticism along the journey, yet he could rest knowing that his path set the cornerstone towards a successful, enduring career. The initial milestones along the path to publication did not just serve as a testament to Koontz's skill but also validated his discovery that stories can indeed enchant and mesmerise forever.

3
Themes of Darkness and Light

Influences from a Troubled Childhood

Family Shadows: Analysing Koontz's Early Environment

Dean Koontz's early life experiences had a profound impact on his thematic preferences, as his personal history possessed defining contours and milestones that influenced the way he told stories. Coming from a problematic family, Koontz was aware of the shadows that could encircle a domestic setting. The dread and uncertainty that permeated his household enriched his writing centred around the exploration of darkness and resilience. His talent for storytelling was rooted in the thorough grasp he possessed of the relations among family members, the inquiry into the consequences of trauma and adversity bequeathed unto the next generation, and the family dynamics scarred by fractured lineage. This deep understanding of human relationships enlightens his readers, offering a unique perspective on the complexities of family life.

The emotional subtleties and deep-seated strife within families became constant motifs in Koontz's stories. The writing of Koontz was deeply influenced by the understanding of people around him, gaining depth from their past and blending it into their stories. His insight into humanity enables him to carve through the cores of family life, revealing the multi-dimensional relationships of love, fear, and hope. The tensions of Koontz's life as a child between light and dark served as an exploration towards understanding the characters' purpose of movement from devastation toward redemption with despair being dealt with in childhood.

With an arresting power, Koontz makes illuminating suggestions for change while capturing the essence of chaotic family structures, reminding people why his stories matter. The enduring mark his past left us invites readers to embrace their deepest struggles and greatest victories, echoing the setting that shaped him. In exposing the contours of deep family shadows, Koontz offers profound insights into the ability of mankind to endure and transform. When his audience willingly steps into the labyrinth of his characters' lives, they have little choice but to grapple with their emotional landscapes, adding to their investment in the story and compassion for the characters' difficulties.

Resilience and Reflection: How Childhood Hardship Shapes Storytelling

Looking into the early years of Dean Koontz's life, it seems his childhood challenges have been expertly interlaced within the pieces of his stories. Facing many challenges and setbacks, Koontz developed a deep inner strength supporting his literary works' underbelly. His arduous struggles burned deep within and gave him a scope for self-reflection, which allowed him to depict human fortitude in the canvas of reality where candles are grasped while walking through the shadows. This characteristic of drawing reflection from one's struggles and projecting it in such a way that demands attention and appreciation has been synonymous with Koontz's identity as a writer. Also, this self-reflective ability has provided room in his works, which calls people to empathise and grasp the beauty within the pain shared by all walks of life. In his brilliantly woven stories, Koontz enables people to believe in the essence of enduring strength within us all, pushing people to face challenges head-on. Through his experiences, he provides people with endless hope, wisdom, and the courage to rediscover themselves.

We cannot dispute that the undaunted spirit born in Koontz's adolescent years continues to influence his stories by adding elements of reflection and resilience, deepening his tales to a transcendence beyond human experience.

Intersecting Paths: Darkness and Redemption in Life and Literature

Surrounded by challenging and unpredictable circumstances, Dean Koontz's childhood became the basis for themes that would later emerge in his writings. Encountering the dualities of redemption and darkness both in real life and literature creates a fascinating narrative that enchants readers across the globe. From the perspective of personal conflict, Koontz depicts a counter-narrative of the struggle and eventual victory where his past meets the light that his novels represent. This universality of his themes creates a sense of connection among his readers, as they recognise their own struggles and victories in his narratives.

The idea of darkness is a multifaceted construct that goes beyond fear and despair. It serves as a medium through which Koontz pays attention to the profound multi-layered intricacies Koontz adds to the condition of humanity in his works through struggles, enduring adversity, and meaningful reflections on life in overwhelming situations. He cites the power of transformative despair and moments of profound darkness from his difficulties. Within those spaces, resilience and hope are nurtured, and confronting one's fears encapsulates an experience of redemption.

On the quest of unearthing concepts of darkness and redemption, Koontz surprisingly bows to the grace of the saddest of all themes; bringing together angels and demons of the human experience, weaving tales that frontally clash with the concept of fighting ordinary inner villains and reaching for light while drowning in obscured joyless reality. The convergence of opposing forces proves the author's capability to create multidimensional characters, letting them endure the conflicts and resolutions that show the unwavering spirit of humanity's fortitude. These characters are not just heroes or villains, but they are complex individuals with their own inner struggles and motivations, making them more relatable and engaging for the readers.

The realms of redemptive arcs in his narratives make Koontz a master of storytelling. He depicts actors who emerge from the depths of despair not unscathed, but transformed and fortified. Koontz's works brilliantly capture the suffering of a single soul trying to fight their way out of the system only to be thrust deeper into a world of blinding light yet pure evil. His mastery of the writing craft demonstrates that facing the cruellest parts of oneself is often the catalyst for real change and that true transformation lies in embracing one's true self. This emphasis on the transformative power of facing one's fears empowers his readers, encouraging them to confront their own inner demons.

This is a clear testament of Koontz's life and how he perceives his personal journey, redemption and darkness serves as the ultimate catalyst for enduring change. In Koontz's works, these themes are not just plot devices, but they are the driving forces behind the characters' actions and the narrative's progression. And this in his writing resonates with the darkness that looms over one's life offering a purpose and drawing from one's self providing an endless spiral of self reflection, giving hope and rebuilding what is shattered which constantly journeys from his haunting history.

The Role of Fear: Harnessing Personal Demons for Creative Fuel

Fear is a factor that "paralyses" a person who seems to have sliced fear the way Koontz weaves the narrative of his life. This well-known name in the world of suspense and horror has, in some way or the other, tried to integrate me into the story of his life.

Every man's journey begins with self-search; if I am not wrong, that is a very painful exercise for Koontz. And suppose you have the self-belief nurtured in your voids, notions of various forms bundled with anxieties. In that case, Koontz appears to be the circus performer who is making the fear part of his world instead of escaping it, simultaneously being brilliant in his mastery of splendid limelight that allows him to litter the fears onto the pages of notes and, afterwards cameras not one but many willingly fasten unto the humans who later on get smothered on understanding the fears of self when clothed in fiction.

Furthermore, Koontz works with fear not just as a form of entertainment but as a form of emotional release for himself and his audience. Koontz imbues readers with the self-confrontation he wishes to achieve by inviting them to embrace their deepest insecurities and fears, providing a collective sense of empathy. This brave self-exploration adds richness to the stories and, more importantly, fiercely connects the author, the story, and the readers far beyond the act of reading.

Most interesting is that Koontz does not use fear as a form of hope but rather the opposite, devoiding his stories of piteous sentiments. Strength and hope are the central themes in his stories—defeated by fear and plunged into despair, only to wait to be redeemed. His intent imbues the ever-present notion of unwavering strength and spirit in bleak situations and furthers the themes intended within his narratives. This facet of his storytelling deepens the almost haphazardly profound mark left on one's mind long after parting with the captivating yet tumultuous journeys found within his pages.

In any case, Koontz's mastery of utilising personal fears as fuel for creativity reveals the transformative nature of art and what it is truly capable of. He is skilled in using fear because it guides him to appreciate and nurture the invisible balance between humanity and the extraordinary, weaving a story beyond any genre. With all these horrifying shocks and victories, Koontz demonstrates the timeless fortitude of the human spirit and provides consolation and encouragement to a world at war with itself in the form of dread and uncertainty.

Symbols of Light: Exploring Optimism Amidst Complex Narratives

Vivid and serene themes do exist, but they are more like an undercurrent in Dean Koontz's storylines, where hope and tranquility are overtaken by dark and chaotic matters. Hope and its essence are best expressed through symbolism, which tends to bring forth light in the form of symbols and metaphors that display humanity's unwavering heroism amidst strife.

In Koontz's narratives, light is more than simply the absence of darkness: it stands for courage, hope, and the innate goodness that people possess. In every kerosene lamp, there is a flickering flame, the dim light of which can be seen fighting against the overwhelming despair, and during the most foreboding of times, a rising sun brings warm, gentle light. Light marks the victory of the human spirit. Koontz deftly uses such symbols throughout his narratives to imbue stories with hope beyond the confines of genre.

In these symbols, Koontz sheds light on the hopefulness of human beings. In his works, the struggle between the two extremes evokes vitality in people and encourages them to transform no matter how hopeless their condition is. Strung out by personal difficulties, characters always reach back to the light that, in this case, represents hope in a desperate world plagued by problems. In such symbols, Koontz builds the tough image of the human mind wherein he gives weight to the so-called light in the dark tunnel of trying times.

The symbolism of light transcends individual characters and integrates into the overarching themes of Koontz's narratives. It is a connecting emblem that brings together different plots and provides them with a shared banner of hope. This balance of dark and light not only enhances the plots in the stories but also demonstrates Koontz's capacity to appeal to the reader's emotions in a very deep way.

Ultimately, the study of symbols in Koontz's stories reveals an intricate form of optimism entwined with other complexities. The symbols of light act as 'polar stars' to navigate the protagonists and readers alike through the maze of obstacles and hardships. Light reminds us that no matter how dark the night is, there is always the hope of dawn—thematically describing why Koontz is a guiding light of hope for many readers throughout his literature.

Literary Catharsis: Emotional Healing Through Fiction

Literature has long served as a vehicle for emotional catharsis, providing both writers and readers with a means to process and heal from profound experiences. For Dean Koontz, the exploration of emotional healing through fiction is not just an aspect, but the essence of his creative endeavours. Through his evocative storytelling, Koontz confronts themes of trauma, loss, and adversity, offering readers an immersive opportunity to navigate these complex emotions. Thus, we need to explore the profound concept of literary catharsis and its transformative power within Koontz's works.

The act of weaving personal turmoil into the lives of fictional characters serves as a therapeutic outlet for authors, enabling them to articulate internal struggles while offering a sense of solace and understanding. Koontz adeptly infuses his protagonists with fragments of his own emotional journeys, intertwining the realms of reality and imagination to construct narratives that resonate on deeply human levels. By acknowledging the universality of pain and resilience, Koontz constructs a bridge between author and reader, fostering an empathetic connection that transcends the boundaries of mere entertainment.

Moreover, encountering characters who grapple with formidable challenges can be profoundly affirming and comforting for readers. The resonance of shared emotional experiences within the pages of a novel offers a form of validation, assuring individuals that they are not alone in their struggles. Koontz's stories delicately navigate the intricacies of emotional healing, interweaving threads of hope, redemption, and inner strength amidst the shadows that loom within his narratives. Within these tales, readers discover a collective space for introspection and solace and a renewed belief in the potential for emotional renewal and growth.

Through literary catharsis, both writer and reader embark on a journey of exploration and enlightenment, transcending the confines of everyday existence to delve into the depths of human emotion. With his mastery of narrative alchemy, Koontz guides audiences through tumultuous landscapes, illuminating the transformative power of embracing vulnerability and confronting inner turmoil head-on.

As such, the journey of emotional healing within Koontz's fiction extends far beyond the mere consumption of a story; it becomes a symbiotic relationship between artist and audience, traversing the intricate terrain of human experience. Literary catharsis allows for the processing of individual tribulations and paves the way for communal empathy, forging connections that echo across time and space. In essence, this profound engagement with emotional catharsis is a testament to the enduring impact of literature as a catalyst for healing and self-discovery. Koontz's narrative tapestries resonate as vibrant testaments to the resilience of the human spirit, inviting readers to embark on an intimate odyssey of emotional restoration and illumination.

Characterisation as Therapy: Personal Struggles Infusing Protagonists

In exploring the realm of storytelling, it becomes evident that authors often imbue their characters with aspects of their struggles. For Dean Koontz, this literary trope has been woven into the fabric of his narratives, manifesting as a form of therapeutic release and transformation. Delving into his works, readers are confronted with protagonists who grapple with inner turmoil, face insurmountable odds, and ultimately find redemption—mirroring the author's journey from adversity to triumph. This deliberate infusion of personal struggles into fictional personas is a testament to the cathartic power of storytelling, where the act of creation becomes a vehicle for emotional expression and introspection.

Koontz's protagonists, in essence, emerge as conduits through which he channels his own experiences, confronting his internal battles within the confines of fictitious worlds while simultaneously offering solace and guidance to his readers. Through meticulous character development, he crafts compelling narrative arcs and conveys profound messages of resilience, hope, and the enduring human spirit. As readers become immersed in these characters' lives, they witness profound emotional journeys and find themselves resonating with the universal struggles encapsulated within these literary embodiments. Indeed, the craft of characterisation as therapy is unequivocally transformative, allowing Koontz to navigate the intricacies of his emotional landscape while fostering profound connections with his audience.

Furthermore, this process elevates his works beyond conventional fiction, infusing them with an authenticity that deeply resonates humanly. By investing his characters with fragments of his vulnerabilities and triumphs, Koontz forges an unbreakable bond between art and artist, inviting readers to embark on a collective odyssey of healing, acceptance, and transcendence. Ultimately, the integration of personal confrontations into the souls of his protagonists renders his narratives not merely as entertaining tales but as intimate reflections of the human condition. This reflection enables the creator and audience to find solace and strength in facing life's formidable trials.

The Dichotomy of Darkness and Hope: Maintaining Balance in Themes

In Dean Koontz's literary realms, the dichotomy of darkness and hope is a guiding force that intricately weaves through his narratives. It is an artful balancing act—a symphony where shadows and light dance in captivating harmony. This delicate equilibrium reflects Koontz's deep understanding of human emotions and the complexities of existence. The interplay between themes of darkness and hope is not merely a narrative device but a profound exploration of the human psyche and the universal struggle between despair and resilience.

Koontz's mastery lies in confronting the darkest aspects of the human condition while infusing his stories with an undeniable undercurrent of hope. It is a testament to his storytelling prowess that he can paint scenes of chilling terror and existential angst yet simultaneously kindle a glimmer of optimism within his readers. This juxtaposition serves as a powerful reflection of reality, for darkness and hope are often inseparable in life. Maintaining this balance amidst polarised themes requires a nuanced approach. Koontz deftly crafts his characters and their journeys with multidimensional layers, portraying their inner conflicts and external challenges with unwavering authenticity. Each triumph over adversity is filled with resonance, breathing life into the eternal struggle against forces seeking to extinguish hope.

Moreover, the dichotomy of darkness and hope serves as a mirror to the human spirit, echoing the universal experience of confronting personal demons and seeking redemption. Through his rich and diverse characters, Koontz provides a canvas for readers to witness the intricacies of human nature, inviting introspection and empathy. By intertwining moments of despair with instances of unwavering courage and compassion, he underscores the enduring power of hope, even in the face of overwhelming darkness. Within this interplay, Koontz's narratives resonate beyond the confines of genre, transcending the mere thrills of suspense and horror. His stories become vessels carrying profound reflections on the human condition, offering readers solace, inspiration, and a renewed sense of fortitude. The delicate equilibrium between darkness and hope in Koontz's narratives serves as a poignant reminder of the profound resilience within each individual, portraying the indomitable spirit that perseveres, no matter how daunting the odds may seem.

Philosophical Reflections: The Broader Human Experience in Writing

As an art form, writing is deeply intertwined with the human experience. Through exploring philosophical themes and existential questions, authors can delve into the core of what it means to be human. Dean Koontz's work exemplifies this profound connection between literature and the human condition. His narratives often serve as mirrors, reflecting the complexities, struggles, and triumphs inherent to our existence.

Here, we aim to deconstruct the philosophical underpinnings of Koontz's storytelling and how they resonate with readers on a universal level. Koontz's writing transcends mere entertainment; it becomes a conduit through which readers can confront their fears, hopes, and moral dilemmas. By weaving intricate narratives exploring the depths of human nature, Koontz invites his audience to dialogue about the fundamental aspects that define us as sentient beings. Whether grappling with themes of identity, destiny, or the balance between good and evil, Koontz's storytelling compels readers to ponder existential questions that transcend time and culture.

Moreover, by addressing these profound concepts, Koontz establishes a profound symbiosis between creator and audience, forging connections that extend far beyond the confines of the printed page. Through philosophical reflections embedded within his works, Koontz offers intellectual stimulation and emotional resonance, inviting readers to embrace a deeper understanding of themselves and the world around them. His narrative craftsmanship serves as a vehicle for introspection, allowing readers to navigate the labyrinthine corridors of the human psyche. Through Koontz's philosophical odyssey, readers are prompted to examine their beliefs, values, and place within the more extraordinary tapestry of humanity. As such, his literary legacy extends beyond mere entertainment, offering a profound and enduring exploration of the broader human experience.

Legacy of Themes: Impact on Readers and Cultural Narrative

Dean Koontz's exploration of themes, particularly the juxtaposition of darkness and light, has significantly impacted readers and contributed to the broader cultural narrative. Through his masterful storytelling, Koontz challenges conventional perspectives and delves into the intricate complexities of the human experience, leaving an enduring imprint on literary discourse and societal consciousness.

Koontz's thematic legacy transcends mere entertainment, as his narratives provoke introspection and encourage critical engagement with the existential dilemmas depicted. The profound impact of his work is evidenced in the profound resonance it elicits within readers from diverse backgrounds, invoking conversations that extend beyond the pages of his books. Furthermore, Koontz's thematic exploration reflects the contemporary cultural landscape, addressing pertinent societal issues while offering avenues for contemplation and discourse. By intertwining darkness and light in his narratives, he sheds light on the intrinsic duality of the human condition, prompting readers to examine their perceptions and beliefs. This engagement with profound themes elevates the cultural narrative, fostering a collective understanding of the intricacies of the human experience and the moral ambiguities inherent in society.

Moreover, the impact of Koontz's themes extends beyond individual readers, permeating the literary and cultural realms at large. His ability to weave thought-provoking narratives that resonate with universal truths contributes to a collective narrative that transcends temporal and spatial boundaries. The enduring relevance of his thematic explorations continues to shape the evolution of literature and the cultural zeitgeist, leaving an indelible mark on future generations of writers and thinkers.

Koontz's thematic legacy enriches the fabric of popular culture, influencing various art forms and mediums. From film adaptations to philosophical discourses, the profound impact of his thematic palette is evident in its far-reaching influence across diverse creative platforms. Through their incorporation into broader cultural narratives, Koontz's themes have catalysed meaningful discussions on morality, resilience, and the eternal struggle between darkness and light. Ultimately, Dean Koontz's legacy of themes serves as a testament to the enduring power of literature to shape perspectives, provoke dialogue, and transcend the bounds of individual narratives. His exploration of darkness and light continues to wield transformative influence, forging an enduring cultural heritage that resonates deeply within the hearts and minds of readers while enriching the broader tapestry of human storytelling and expression.

4
Crafting the Uncategorisable

The Blending of Genres

Understanding Genre Blending

The genre-blending aspect of literature is one of the most dynamic and complex since it is beyond the boundaries of conventional literature. Within the scope of this book, we look at the rationale behind the author's persisting challenge of merging traditional genre lines into plot lines that resist conventional categorisation. One must be familiar with the complexities encased within multiple literary forms to analyse vision genre-blending and ready to step beyond traditional narrative limits. The author's desire to offer a transcendental experience that breaks free from the confines of the singular genres laid out by publishers serves as the primary motivation for blending genres. This leads to the portrayal of themes and characters in a more layered, sophisticated, and rich manner, thus allowing the creation of narratives that accommodate audiences from all walks of life.

Blending genres poses significant challenges, such as maintaining order and reason within the flow of the jarringly mixed components from different genres. Also, the author faces the issue of expectation and reception from audiences and critics accustomed to rigid genre boundaries. The author manages these challenges while remaining committed to developing stories that no longer adhere to genre classification's conventional labels and boundaries.

This chapter will illuminate the author's creative process and endeavour to blend genres, thereby fostering a deeper connection with the readers and their appreciation of the intricate complexity of constructing plots that transcend the conventional limits of literature.

Grasping the Boundaries of Literary Works

Boundaries in literature are the borders that divide and control peculiar markers within specific literary genres. These boundaries, often defined by the conventions and expectations of a particular genre, are informative to authors because they seek to devise narratives which aim at transgressing the norm or attempt to defy the prevailing literary convention. Knowledge of the boundaries which are taken for granted in different genres provides the authors with the opportunity to move across and combine different components into a cohesive whole. Most importantly, the inter-relationship network of genres allows different motifs to be addressed and to appeal to a wider audience.

The comprehension of genre tropes enables the authors to defy expectations and provide their readers with an experience that escapes the limits of a single genre. This serves to enhance the storytelling processes in addition to the fact that it accelerates the development of literature as an art by introducing new dimensions of imagination.

Understanding boundaries in literature allows the authors to create certain levels of conflict and congruence among various genres, providing the grounds for combining different elements into one captivating narrative.

Writing in such manners enables authors to capture the spirits of various genres while providing spirited and imaginative reading experiences for their audiences. This is why understanding and crossing literary boundaries emerge and matter, fostering a colourful and limitless literary world that knows no bounds.

Influences from Gothic and Mystery Traditions

The influence of gothic and mystery on Dean Koontz's work is profound and sophisticated. It shapes how he narrates stories and enriches his literary works. Koontz's incorporation of gothic and mystery elements is marked by a deep understanding and appreciation of the traditions set by earlier literary masters, from eerie settings and darkly lit moods to enigmatic characters and perplexing plots.

Koontz's narratives reflect the influence of gothic literature in their supernatural focus, providing a sense of haunting mystery and suspense while underscored by the macabre. The shadowy, dilapidated hallways of the ancient structures in his tales often serve as beautiful backdrops for his stories brimming with existential dread and psychological turmoil. Oppressive landscapes, decaying mansions, and enigmatic strangers are recurring elements within his tale, which form a captivating, riddled sense of dread and mystery that mesmerises and draws readers into the narrative.

Furthermore, the use of mystery traditions within his works serves to heighten the complexity of his storytelling and the intrigue in his works. He employs classic mystery concepts like intricate puzzles, morally ambiguous characters, and a lack of clues to craft intricately designed webs of ever-heightening suspense that keep readers guessing until the final page. Koontz also pays homage to renowned mystery authors, celebrating the art of misdirection, skillfully guiding readers through intricate paths of uncertainty, and revealing them to a world of thrilling possibility.

Koontz's narratives' captivating gothic and mystery blend deeply examines human consciousness, morality, and the concept of reality itself. Combining strange and mysterious elements unlocks Koontz's exploration of existential dread, moral conflicts, and the ongoing battle between good and evil. He crafts stories without the restrictions of a single genre by merging these traditional literary elements, inviting readers into realms where the lines separating reality from fiction blur and power rests in enigmatic forces from the unknown.

Appreciating the intricate fusion of gothic and mystery influences in Koontz's works helps us understand the strengths and weaknesses of his narrative voice's differing traditions.

Using Elements of Science Fiction

Balancing imagination and plausibility when incorporating science fiction elements into a narrative is crucial. Speculative science, futuristic technologies, and alternative universes inform the creative mind. They also transcend the boundaries of imagination. Science fiction has always been a rich canvas supporting traditional literary boundaries. Koontz is famously known for blending genres of literature in a single piece, so it serves as no surprise that he introduces layers of deep narratives to his counter-science fiction. Through the scientific exploration of advanced concepts, the imagination of dystopian worlds, and extraterrestrial civilisations, it is impossible not to notice the charm of science fiction that Koontz has used in mastery. It is crucial to focus on extensive research needed to ground elements of speculation so that they do not come off as absurd, thus improving the reader's experience and suspension of disbelief. Immersion and suspension of disbelief are crucial to the modern reader, and through vivid descriptions and carefully crafted worlds, Koontz builds scientifically grounded yet fantastical worlds. Combined with softer approaches, the use of science fiction elements gives him the power to delve into the most profound philosophical questions about humanity, morality, and the repercussions of technological development.

This kind of depth offers a new dimension to his stories for readers who want something other than entertainment. With science fiction elements, Koontz can weave complex and layered plots that force his characters to face the unexplainable and move through the unexplainable. The genre's capacity for creative imagination allows Koontz to stretch the limits of the imagination, forcing readers to think about what the universe holds.

With other genres such as horror, suspense, and mystery, Koontz combines them with science fiction to create stories without any definite boundaries, thus giving various options to different types of readers. This combination of genres expands his options for telling stories and shows his work's creativity and intelligence. So, in other words, adding science fiction factors allows him to shape his stories with awe, hypothesising and stimulating her mentally, thus appealing to people emctionally and thoughtfully.

Suspension and Thrill in Storytelling

Suspense and thrill are vital to storytelling. These twc elements serve as the heart that drives stories forward. They also shock audiences. In Dean Koontz's works, suspenseful and thrilling elements go beyond entertainment as he seeks to explore human emotions and the human condition. Koontz masterfully employs these elements to capture his readers' attention and to offer readers an immersive experience full of tension, anticipation, and excitement. He achieves a delicate balance of pace, revelation, and atmosphere, allowing the reader to be thrilled and propelled toward the story's peak. The application of suspense and thrills is a painstakingly honed artistic endeavour, and Koontz wields his skill in such art with great precision. His works are rich with suspenseful and in:ricate details that are carefully threaded within the storyline. Also, these elements allow him to put forth significant issues, dilemmas, and themes that force readers to engage in deep philosophical reflection instead of simply escaping from reality.

As readers navigate through the author's heart-stopping, pulsating sequences, they are made to confront their fears, desires, and even moral dilemmas, resulting in a deeper engagement with the narrative. Koontz demonstrates his unrivalled genius through this careful manipulation of the suspenseful and thrilling, earning his place as one of the earliest fiction practitioners who defies categorisation. He reshapes the field of telling stories by attempting to deepen the examination of suspense and thrill as an opportunity for intellectual reflection, emotional connection, and transcendental questioning. His claim to fame—the power of suspense and thrill as tools to dazzle and insight reflection—is a testament to the phenomenon of literature Koontz masterfully reveals, claiming dominion over and far surpassing the boundaries of his genre.

Exploration of Psychological Depths

The psychological exploration within literature serves the purpose of creating a profound connection between the story and the reader. Every plot revolves around emotional turmoil, interpersonal friction, and ethical issues, which form the foundation of the character's evolution and the intricate changes in the plot. The multiple characters that Dean Koontz creates are a testament to how he explores the extreme depths of one's psyche. His writings demonstrate a keen insight into human thinking and feeling. With vivid and acute self-reflection, he places upon his readers a challenge to confront their fears and desires as they undertake a journey into the human psyche. The readers are not mere spectators, but active participants, presented with characters as passengers on the voyage of the unknown self who are exploring the borders of madness and battling the lurking darkness. This interdependence of fear, hope and the basic need to be understood depicts the relationships in his works and draws the readers' attention far beyond mere storytelling.

Koontz's integration of psychology into stimulating, mysterious, and speculative fiction far surpasses entertainment, achieving levels of profound introspection. These forms of storytelling, while entertaining, encourage readers to empathise with the psychological battlegrounds within the characters' minds rather than the themes overtly presented. This multi-layered approach shapes narratives that imprint enduring impressions in the minds of readers, leaving a lasting mark. Thus, the capacity to explore psychology within a story attests to Koontz's command of literature beyond particular genres. The result is an engaging and deeply touching work of literature.

Creating Smooth Transitions Between Genres

Developing a plot that blends different genres is a complex undertaking. It requires mastery of thematic storytelling. Blending two or more genres into a single piece of art or literature requires a full understanding of the norms associated with each genre and the creativity to twist or merge them into something new. A prolific narrator of combined genres is Dean Koontz, who mixes elements of horror, suspense, science fiction, and psychological thrillers into works that defy genre classification.

One of the most important techniques for blending varied genres is to use differing pacing and tonal shifts simultaneously. By varying the rhythm of the story and switching from tense, pensive to highly intense, visceral action, the author strives for a boundless reading experience. This fluid construction breaks the confines of traditional genres. Such ease enables the reader to avoid jarring cuts while shifting between genres.

Multifaceted characters and complex plotlines play a crucial role in integrating different genres in Dean Koontz's works. His characters are deep and complex, and their transformational journeys traverse diverse thematic landscapes, allowing for varying genre influences to be woven into the narrative fabric. This singular unifying element provides a cohesive structure that seamlessly integrates the elements of horror, suspense, science fiction, and psychological thrillers into works that defy genre classification.

Moreover, applying symbols, metaphors, and allegories enables genre shifts by providing core thematic elements that resonate across different genres. The author employs particular symbols or metaphors that form a unified narrative language, surpassing a specific genre's boundaries and inviting readers to engage with the story on various interpretative levels.

Atmospheric world-building and rich details create a contextual foundation for smooth transitions between different genres. The author anchors the narrative within a vividly realised, atmospherically rich, and unique setting that provides a stage for the disparate genre elements, enhancing the narrative's overall coherence and immersive impact.

As stated previously, the ability to transcend the boundaries of different genres enables writers to test, innovate, and redefine the scope of literature while taking the readers on a journey through different thematic waves. In the hands of an adept storyteller such as Dean Koontz, blending genres becomes an example of the limitless nature of literature and calls on readers to appreciate works beyond the confines of a single genre.

Audience Reception and Critical Perception

The reception from an audience and how a critic perceives a work are essential elements when assessing the impact of blending literary genres. The combination of different genres within a single text likely provokes mixed feelings, especially from readers and critics, some of whom appreciate the integration. In contrast, others struggle to adapt to the unfamiliar storytelling paradigms. Additionally, perception reception is multi-faceted, and different levels of readers have different attitudes toward specific literary pieces. For example, die-hard fans from particular genres may approach hybrid texts with scepticism regarding how their beloved conventions will blend with other literary traditions. Conversely, more eclectic readers view genre-bending narratives as invigorating and intellectually stimulating, celebrating their unpredictable and rule-defying character.

Furthermore, genre-bending literature requires such literary analysis and considers critical perception, focusing on the impact of such works being accepted or neglected in the literary context. It assumes the functions of critics and literary reviewers who examine the components and themes in detail and their relevance in literature. They assess the effectiveness of genre inclusion, the fluidity of transitions between discordant narrative parts, and the reader's intellectual and emotional engagement.

Moreover, the critique further examines the impact of contemporary culture and society on the blending of literary genres and how these stories reflect, challenge, or reinforce accepted narratives and values. Critics also reflect on the possible impacts of these works on the future of literature to further understand their importance in the literary world. At the same time, it is important to recognise the subjective nature of reception and criticism. For instance, genre-blending stories can be meaningful and enjoyable for some, while for others, crossing literary borders will be incomprehensible. Furthermore, critical judgments may be as enthusiastic as issuing condemnation for bold innovation or as harsh as praising the lack of innovation. Hence, the discussion on reception and criticism is a vivid illustration of the dialogue between the vision, expectations, and judgment of the creators. In conclusion, offering a well-rounded analysis of audience reception and critical perception adds nuance to the discussion on genre-blending literature. It highlights the need to go beyond conventional boundaries and challenge consideration of the transformation of literature.

Challenges and Innovations in Genre Hybridity

For writers looking to expand the borders of storytelling, genre hybridity offers challenges to overcome and opportunities to innovate. Perhaps one of the greatest hurdles is the possibility of backlash from traditional fetishists who have a distinct and simplistic view of genres and their roots. Writers attempting genre hybrids have to navigate the honouring and subverting of age-old traditions in a way that produces something new and captivating. This balancing act demands a mastery of the tangles of each genre being fused and how these tangles interact with and enhance one another. In addition, the dilemma of not sufficiently pleasing fans of a single genre is still at large, as expectations most certainly differ from one literary culture to another.

However, rich avenues for innovative thought and imagination could offset the lack of universally accepted solutions. Through the skilful blending of these genres, authors can create stories that stretch the limits of the individual genre and cross into new realms of expression, thereby creating impactful narrative responses for people from all walks of life.

This synthesis process creates new literary worlds that do not yet exist. These worlds are created by combining and remixing familiar tropes and concepts in unrecognised manners that are provocative and refreshing for audiences to consume. Moreover, the fusion of different styles in a single piece of literature makes it possible for unorthodox concepts and themes to be introduced into mainstream literature while provoking ideas and expanding the possibilities of what can be done within the art of storytelling.

Addressing these problems within a multi-genre context requires much planning and execution. As in all aspects of genre hybridity, seamless integration requires a thorough understanding of each genre's principles alongside the ability to spot unifying features. Adding multiple genres poses a challenge as finding where to strike a balance is elusive without overwhelming the impact of individual components, thus requiring mastery and artistry. One must focus on resolving the clash caused by different genres because rough changes or mismatched themes spoil the infiltrating experience offered by a good book.

This search for variety in genres brings about courageous efforts and ventures to cross-set boundaries of traditional literature and the art of storytelling, thus offering endless possibilities.

This requires an unwavering dedication to craftsmanship, a steadfast zeal for innovation, and a deep appreciation for blended traditions. Your hybridity combines multiple genres. It is complex and yet rewarding. Literature creates infinite possibilities and encourages writers to explore and reinvent as they try to trace their unique mark within the world of stories.

Conclusion: Constructing a Distinctive Narrative Voice

In dealing with the challenges and innovations of genre hybridity, it seems that the attempted integration or blending of genres results in the emergence of a unique narrative voice. This observation underscores the importance of individualistic storytelling forms, which strongly reflects the above analysis. With every attempt that writers make to merge two or more opposing genres, they inevitably develop their unique style of writing, which adds to the rich literary expression.

A distinctive narrative voice transforms storytelling into an art form. First, It is achieved by combining different and often unrelated themes, characters, and plots. Having set this goal, a writer embarks on a most challenging task. The task requires striking balance and harmony. The achievement of all the above results in a narrative without a clear genre.

Furthermore, the defining of a distinct narrative voice involves the comprehension and application of literary conventions. In each genre, authors have to follow certain established rules. However, if an author decides to break the rules creatively and preserve the genre's spirit, they can go beyond the borders of imagination. Such rule-breaking provides an opportunity to forge narratives that form a bond of connection and detachment within the readers, providing an unparalleled experience and delivering a form of lasting impression that integrates enchantment and arrest on numerous dimensions.

Crafting a distinctive narrative voice requires a sophisticated understanding of how audiences respond and interact with texts. While bending the rules of genre fusion, authors must pay attention to what the readers expect and want. There is a great achievement in striking this balance, which is rather difficult, as it opens new avenues for stories that appeal to people from many walks of life while crossing boundaries of expectations set around genres and literary forms. In this case, the challenge is that rote expectation and rule-dominated thinking are precisely where many readers get stuck and that very shackles are what profound literature seeks to break.

Defining an individual narrative voice elucidates the height of cross-genre amalgamation and innovation in literature. It illustrates the power of storytelling in ways that go beyond the defined parameters of genres. Authors can change the meaning of telling stories by creating new worlds filled with deep characters and complex plots, permanently transforming the literature landscape and adding value to it with their unparalleled signature as distinct as fingerprints.

5
Whispers and Breakthroughs

Achieving Literary Success

Early Career Challenges and Perseverance

Koontz had to face multiple efforts when he started venturing into writing. It is reported that he did not give up on his passion for writing despite having setbacks in life. His aggressive pursuit ended up blazing the path for him towards significant success later in his life. Author Dean

Koontz openly shares his struggles as a 'failed' writer before hitting it big. Koontz mentions in his biography how having no backup plans paid off when he buckled down and pursued his dreams without giving up. He believes that having this level of focus leads to great fulfilment in life as long as it is paired with relentless execution. Whatever he started doing became easier and provided the fulfilment he craved. It was in his early 20s that Koontz learnt that failure after failure is a stepping stone towards success.

The Turning Point: Whispers of Talent Recognised

Dean Koontz sought his place in the literary world, and as any author will tell you, the path is riddled with challenges. This moment came in the unconventional form of recognition that served as a monument to mark the beginning of his career. Koontz's continuous hard work as an author was finally paying off.

This event changed the quality of work he could hope to produce and obtain recognition for. The powerful impressiveness of admiring shrieks cut loose the boundaries of the twiddling temptations of the author's amplified expectations of a warm reception by readers and leading critics. With an expanding readership, a new world opened to Koontz, and the author no longer needed to expect adulation; he could bathe in it.

The turning point justified Koontz's commitment to refining his skills, further reinforcing his conviction in his imagination and storytelling prowess. It also provided long-overdue affirmation while encouraging him to explore the limits of his creative expression.

As murmurs of recognition reached a deafening applause, Koontz led the charge of a new literary zeitgeist. His ability to captivate audiences with compelling narratives was his marquee, which has already earned him a place among the greats of fiction. This significant turning point in Koontz's literary journey was the start of the profound mark he was destined to carve in literature, establishing a legacy that would stand the test of time.

First Shimmer of Recognition: Gaining Momentum

In Dean Koontz's case, the first flashes of recognition came during his early writing career. He was regarded as a star in the making due to his dedication to storytelling and writing in general. Koontz possessed the rare talent of crafting story after story of interesting characters and gripping plots that would make literary circles let out early whispers of praise. Koontz had captured the attention of many with his talent for imagination and writing long before he came out with his brand, be it through early novels or short stories.

While mastering his craft, he began tackling the intricacies of the publishing world. He networked with agents and publishers and marketed himself strategically to broaden his reach, knowing the scope and impact of his work well. This period marked an important turning point, as his publishing and marketing strategies would prove critical for his future achievements.

Like Koontz's other pursuits, earning literary recognition came with its own set of challenges and successes. His dedication to producing quality literature that is not confined to a single genre marked him in a highly competitive market. With his growing recognition came a heightened anticipation for new releases, generating buzz within the literary world. Through meticulous planning and relentless effort, Koontz secured a position in the industry, building a strong foundation for what would later become a legendary career.

Strategic Publishing Choices and Market Positioning

As far as literary accomplishments are concerned, strategic publishing decisions substantially impact the career trajectory of an author. By invigorating market demand, Koontz positively positioned himself, utilising his remarkable skills as a spellbinding storyteller who could enthral readers of all genres. Leaving no stone unturned, Koontz self-consciously ensured that his decisions covetously synced with both the spirit of the times and the latent wish of the audience. He blended creativity with shrewdness through strategic decisions in themes, characters, and narration styles, ensuring his literary works appealed to the changing publishing world.

Dramatic shifts in Koontz as an author started to take place considering market segmentation and positioning. Seizing this opportunity, he immediately started to address the varying tastes of different groups of readers without sacrificing his artistic integrity. This insight allowed him to widen his market appeal dynamically and unexpectedly build a strong and loyal readership, thus earning him a reputation as a literary innovator whose writings defy boundaries and fuse genres.

Koontz manoeuvred strategically regarding genre orientation or the way one views the genre, balancing his works to seek greater attention while preserving the core and inventiveness of his stories. This type of movement within the publishing profession helped him achieve fame, which subsequently brought him some amount of permanent success.

On another note, Koontz's strategy considered the individual projects, his lifelong career, and his professional sustainability. In light of new innovations such as technology, he rethought promotional methods and shifted his approach to the ever-changing publishing scene. He made sure that his narratives would be in the hands of the audience in or through more innovative ways. He changed how he presented his stories, which not only enhanced his audience but made him a daunting force within the industry.

Through shrewd promotional tactics and dealings with publishers and agents, Koontz emerged as a dominant force in literature while expertly manoeuvring through the complexities of the publishing world. To a great extent, he made choices that blended creativity with commercial logic, achieving a refined balance that boosted his reputation as a writer. His exceptional skill in harnessing available publishing prospects with insightful planning illustrated the importance of making decisions to achieve literary prominence.

Compelling Narratives That Captivate

Telling inspiring stories is fundamental to literary artistry among writers. This sophisticated skill goes beyond skillfully intertwining plotlines with well-developed characters and evocative settings. Koontz masterfully implements this principle by continuously surpassing the expectations of his audience through genre-defying gripping tales that evoke empathy.

Suspense and Koontz's Narratives have a unique relationship (aka one of the unique features of Koontz's narratives is the way he weaves suspense and tension masterfully). From the psychological depths of a thick-threaded thriller to the spine-chilling extremes of horror fiction, Koontz's storytelling dominates the minds and retinas of readers long after they have finished reading the book.

Additionally, the nature of Koontz's characters emotes profound portions of richness to the stories. Every character comes alive and helps readers visualise the ugly truth that lies hidden under the exquisite surface. Each character is extremely relatable, suffering flaws such as being ex-gambling casino addicts dealing with their sordid battles, complex anti-heroes fuelled by their passionate convictions, not sane enough to step out of the pages, but sane enough to be deeply memorable.

Aside from character and plot, the impact of his narratives is amplified by how he captures detail through the setting. Every one of his settings enhances the depth and texture of his entire story, such as atmosphere-packed terrains and skillfully crafted scenes from tortured cities. The world crafted by Koontz is so vividly real that in conjunction with the surrounding contexts, the readers can immerse themselves in ever-evolving fictional events.

Devoid of overage, knotty themes alongside riveting plots are also present within Koontz's literature, propelling readers into thought-provoking debates. Be it the exposition of whimsical features of the human heart, beset with panic-hero necrology contemplation, or the internal war between good and bad, readers are always invited to challenge themselves philosophically.

He has strived to leave an everlasting mark in readers' hearts by harnessing emotions and changing their perspectives through emotion-shifting stories. It no longer comes as a surprise when one's perspective of Koontz changes after reading the creative blend of plot, character, setting, individuality, and theme, as it is a testament to the power of storytelling.

Critical Acclaim and Popular Acceptance

At the onset of Dean Koontz's literary career, achieving critical acclaim and popular acceptance were significant benchmarks to work towards. With each new release by Koontz, there was a likelihood that the book could become a classic (in its own right) and receive both popular and critical acclaim. The public admiration and critical acknowledgement of Koontz's works were the hallmarks of his exceptional talent and skill. Regardless of the book he was working on, a chilling suspense novel or a deep reflection of humanity, Koontz was guaranteed to succeed in astounding readers and receiving the respect of critics and colleagues alike.

Koontz's path to critical acclaim was paved with recognition of his masterful psycho-thriller writing, his distinctive narrative voice, and his complex and imaginative inventiveness. His creative style, which transcended the boundaries of any one genre, earned him the respect of literary circles as a true innovator. This praise for Koontz was not confined to a single book; his name became synonymous with literature and creativity, a symbol of his unique and pioneering approach to storytelling.

Koontz's storytelling resonated with a wide range of readers, contributing to his broad popular acceptance. His skilful weaving of intricate plots, multifaceted characters, and captivating ideas drew readers from all walks of life into the immersive worlds he meticulously constructed.

The universal appeal of his works, embraced by readers of all ages, genders, and cultures, is a testament to Koontz's ability to connect with diverse audiences.

Furthermore, the synergy of critical acclaim and popular acceptance Koontz received highlighted the significance of his impact on literature. As Koontz's popularity among the readership evolved positively, so did the literary accolades appearing throughout his career. His works were celebrated, from the bestseller lists to receiving literary honours, which continued to mark him as a luminary of the written word.

In the end, the enduring legacy of Dean Koontz, marked by the convergence of popular acceptance with critical acclaim, not only strengthened his standing as a prolific author but also showcased the impact of his exceptional storytelling talents. This legacy positions him alongside contemporaries in the literary canon, inspiring countless generations of writers and readers alike and inviting us to appreciate his significant contributions to literature.

Adapting to Change: Embracing New Trends

For a literary figure, understanding the trends and preferences of readers always has to be on their radar. A paradigm shift in writing style, themes, and even telling stories must be adapted to engage with audiences and develop the genre. With the rapid technological advancement and change in the types of readers, keeping a balance between the conventional and innovative has to be maintained to stir the audience's interest. This part explores how various well-known writers have adapted emerging trends into their timeless narratives to harmonise the fundamentals of classic literature with modern innovation.

There is an increasing acceptance of embracing multicultural and diverse perspectives in narratives as modern literature aligns towards its more progressive essence. Today's writers are tapping into inclusivity by extending the scope of characters and experiences to capture a wider audience. Authors use social awareness and compassionate stories to embrace the diversity of cultures, races, and genders, reflecting the human experience.

The emergence of new technologies has transformed the distribution of literature, requiring authors to adapt to new platforms and mediums. Embracing these trends involves making use of digital storytelling, interactive narratives, and transmedia approaches that appeal to contemporary audiences through multi-sensory engagement. The use of augmented reality, podcasts, and interactive e-books are multimedia elements that allow authors to transcend traditional constraints and reach readers in new and innovative ways. This shift in storytelling methods invites us to be excited and open-minded about the future of literature.

The need to address critical global challenges and socio-political issues within literature has also motivated the rise of socially conscious fiction. Authors are venturing beyond the boundaries of traditional literature to create works that both entertain and provoke critical dialogue on important societal issues. Through environmental conservation, mental health advocacy, and social justice discourse, these authors align their works with today's societal consciousness, strengthening their literature's impact and relevance.

Coping with modifications and employing new changes is a quintessential fusion of honouring literary traditions and stoking the fire of creativity. Accomplished authors always pay attention to new themes and viewpoints through the lens of storytelling skills. This kind of flexibility not only preserves position in the literary world but also fosters new opportunities for growth and changes in the narrative world.

The Impact of Early Works on Genre Evolution

Dean Koontz's initial work is often perceived as the first block of the building that constitutes his literary works. His early works seem to leave an imprint on every fictional genre, shaping and popularising popular fiction. Further contemplating the details of these elementary works elucidates how much they shaped the prevailing literature culture, inviting us to appreciate his significant influence.

One remarkable feature of the author's earlier pieces is how they escape all possible frameworks. These stories converged and prepared for far more later in storytelling, for which the author was later famous, ontogenetically advanced and liberated genre fiction so that more sophisticated and combining stories could spontaneously develop. Perhaps it would be no exaggeration to claim that the author's captivating works from the first years of his literary career mostly ensured that the readers' imagination was mutated for a new era of renaissance in literature that needed little foundation and much in its wild form.

The emotional and aesthetic aspects latent in the author's early writings also contributed to setting standards due to the thematic contours they embraced. These profound fictions appealed deeply regarding human experience, fears, and hopes. This new augmentation of literary value within genre fiction improved the author's reputation and set off a process of redialling audience expectations for more complex and deeply engaging popular fiction. An additional salient influence of the author's early works stems from their function as forerunners to some of literature's most persistent and recognisable motifs and archetypes. The characters, themes, and even narrative structures that are within these original texts have, over time, become part of the reader's and writer's shared culture. The fact that these components persist across later works has also helped cement the author's reputation as a pioneer whose imaginative work still echoes in the leaps and bounds of modern literature.

In summary, the author's early works are seminal in creating and developing so many literary genres that one would be hard-pressed to argue otherwise. His impact on the enrichment and diversification of popular fiction and its storytelling frameworks positions the author as a prominent benchmark whose creative footprints are still felt in contemporary literature.

Establishing a Distinctive Voice in Literature

In literature, creating a unique voice is synonymous with creating a 'brand' for oneself in storytelling. This is something that Dean Koontz has been working on through the process of self-reflection and, in his own words, journeying. Even in his early career years, he had the habit of trying to write stories that blended multiple genres, including suspense, horror, sci-fi, and even insight into deep humanity. The way he approached the boundaries of genres was truly magnificent and showed his willingness to break into a very tight niche in literature. Looking back at his works, Koontz's unique voice appears to come from the complex weave of the tapestry of deep themes, rich and intricate characters, and, most importantly, his will to make the readers feel or think, preferably both. Something that stands out in Koontz's writing is the remarkable ability to turn mundane settings into spectacles, drawing the reader into a realm where the lines between reality and fantasy are beautifully blurred. Such an approach makes the audience unable to turn their eyes away, and at the same time, it reiterates the notion that he can go beyond the borders of traditional genres. The unique tone of Koontz's style bears witness to the sadness with which he depicts his characters' struggles, victories, and moral complexities.

As readers embark on their journeys, they face some of the most daunting issues concerning ethics, the human spirit, and the ongoing conflict between good and evil. As Koontz advanced in his career, he became determined to maintain a distinct voice, prompting him to seek unexplored pathways, thus chronologically reinforcing the progression of stories. Whether diving deep into the psychology of the antagonist or constructing elaborate suspense, all his writings have stubbornly resisted the pull of subservience. Moreover, Koontz's works' moral focus and richness of themes demonstrate his committed resolve to elevate the form to something beyond mere entertainment. In doing so, he entertains while stimulating thought over the issues of existence, society, and the elusive reality of life. The rise and lasting impact of Koontz's distinguishing voice in the literature demonstrates his pioneering approach to contemporary fiction in a way that defies classification, branding him a universal figure in literature and imprinting his name indelibly in the hearts and minds of countless readers.

Reflecting on Achievement: A Launchpad for Future Success

The achievement of literary prowess is a testament to one's life, shaping the future along the lines of relentless efforts. Success is a journey, engendering a perspective that there lies much to achieve in the forthcoming years and as an author, there rests an entire arena of exploration. This commerce guides trusting and touching experiences in an individual's life, which, at every corner tilt, has every plan working in parallel, keeping in mind the struggles and achievements that have paved the way towards the author's career. Echoing within are the ample resounding impacts attributed to one's personality, which garners special attention from all readers, suggesting that each tale told has become part of the reader's record through reminiscence, not just fiction. Further, this strengthens the author's resolve not to bend the spine of the literary books until the boundaries of imagination are exceeded while hoping. Additionally, recognition serves as the opening to classroom floors, allowing for the highlighting of crucial initiatives and telling stories that fight for the help sought through paving words.

Through reflection, this chapter acknowledges the burden of responsibility that comes with success, compelling the author to remain devoted to storytelling while preserving the particular creative aspect that distinguishes them. The success helps foster development and encourages the author to transform in ways that captivate audiences constantly in flux. Accomplishments remind the author that they do not provide room for complacency, and a constant search for the reinvention of self is needed to build a legacy marked by excellence. With this realisation, the author dares to take on undisputed subjects, employ non-chronological order in telling the story, and challenge the expectations of the genre to lay the foundation for future successes. Reflection on achievement captures the power of storytelling and urges the author to broaden the scope of what is possible in literature. As an author, life's mission is to write stories that endure and leave a mark for future generations, ensuring that an author's journey outlasts any present victories.

6

The Odd Thomas Phenomenon

A Beloved Character Enters the Scene

The Genesis of Odd Thomas: Conception and Creation

The making of Odd Thomas by Dean Koontz is a captivating odyssey into the spirit of creativity. The genesis of Odd Thomas is a product of multifarious influences, experiences, and imaginations blended. When creating Odd, Koontz wished for a remarkable character to which an average person could relate. Therefore, he drew inspiration from real people, people from the society around him, and even from the author's many self-reflective thoughts. This relatability of Odd Thomas, a character who is not perfect but deeply human, is what draws readers in and keeps them engaged.

The uniqueness of Koontz's creation lies in his deft execution of a character who possesses extraordinary empathy, perception, and the ability to deeply feel others' emotions. As an anthropocentric character, Odd's ability to see spirits that refuse to leave and his endless quest for justice is heightened by supernatural influence. Such traits enrich and give depth to the character of Odd Thomas, who is multifarious and possesses assets alien to the world of fiction and fantasy.

As Koontz worked on the early drafts of Odd Thomas, he painstakingly fleshed out a morally complex and achingly self-flawed character whose enchanting qualities were but the tip of the iceberg. The development of Odd's quirks mirrors Koontz's attempts toward crafting a protagonist whose intricacies would connect with readers at a much deeper level. While developing Odd's character, Koontz set out to create a symbol of hope amidst hardship that represents the strength of humanity's spirit.

The founding steps of Odd Thomas show his care for characters like Odd, who do not fit neatly into boxes. By designing Odd as a character who is simultaneously deeply flawed and courageously virtuous, Koontz ensured that Odd would charm readers worldwide and win them over repeatedly. These ideas and designs are solely the product of Koontz's amazing skill in blending human realities with highly subjective values and beautifully compelling narratives.

Character Analysis: Odd's Distinct Voice and Perspective

Odd Thomas's distinctive voice and perspective, the central character in Dean Koontz's series, set him apart in literature. He introspectively expresses his thoughts and feelings profusely, recounting his life experiences in a manner that almost all readers could relate to. This unique perspective, coupled with Odd's compelling narrative voice, is what intrigues and captivates readers, drawing them into his world.

Another fascinating aspect is Odd's ability to seamlessly blend more than one genre into his stories. Even though the series takes a darker, spookier direction with supernatural elements and suspenseful storylines, Odd's narrative voice brings each story to life with compassion and optimism. This skilful blending of genres, from horror to mystery, adds a layer of entertainment and engagement that keeps readers hooked.

Through Odd's eyes, readers encounter an intricate mix of themes, including loss, the profound concept of love, and the unfathomable idea of destiny.

Since life and death are often shrouded in the inexplicable, Odd's thoughts enter the realm of contemplation. He creates an array of resonating emotions, meshing deeply with readers even after the last word has been read. The unfathomable winds of compassion and bravery encircle readers through Odd's character. His unbending perspective of morality and fierce commitment to safeguarding the defenceless Kindle inspire even after the darkest moments.

Moving on to Odd, he contradicts traditional moulds. His structure remains the opposite, showcasing him as a real human being steeped in imperfections. The very claims of self-doubt and perseverance woven into the personality render him relatable. Such a paradoxical character allows readers to forge a bond during their inspirational journey. In detail, Dean Koontz has carefully crafted popular character sketches that span beyond the boundaries of novels and dominate the hearts of numerous fans.

Literary Devices: Blending Horror, Mystery, and Heart

The Odd Thomas series by Dean Koontz illustrates the author's skilful use of literary devices that heighten the reading experience. Koontz entraps the reader with a story that combines horror, mystery, and emotion, goes beyond a single genre, and simultaneously incorporates many genres. This combination fosters an engaging experience for the readers on different emotional and intellectual dimensions, concentrated and dispersed simultaneously.

Within the boundaries of horror, Koontz builds up a feeling of suspense with tangible fear, which keeps the reader interested paragraph after paragraph. Encounters with the evil and supernatural are described in such vivid detail that they give the story a spooky and creepy feel. Such horror in the story describes his world wrapped in its setting. Certainly, all this is bound to draw the reader into Odd Thomas's intrigue.

The skilful construction of mysteries alongside the plot makes the storyline more interesting. Koontz's artistry makes the readers part of the story when they try to solve the mysteries concealed with clues and misleading hints. With mysteries embedded with Koontz's brilliant attention, every clue provided raises the uncertainty about whether it will be the answer to the questions or not.

Suspense and curiosity intertwine to give shape to a narrative that captures the mind and imagination, ensuring a truly captivating and engrossing experience.

Apart from the elements of suspense and mystery, there is an infusing of love, loss, and redemption that adds great emotional weight to the story. Emotions while dealing with human beings by nature would occur in real life, and such a touching and relatable narrative greatly contributes to the readers. This allows the readers to warm their hearts with the events surrounding Odd Thomas' life.

Horror and mystery — blended with heartwarming tales — synergistically meld to give way to entertainment, but for Koontz, it serves as an important prophetic commentary of humanity. The absolute brilliance of his endless creativity of the world and people within the pages of his books is a strong testament to the fascinating strength of his storytelling.

Cultural Impact: Odd Thomas in Popular Culture

The impact of Dean Koontz's character, Odd Thomas, has been immense, affecting many areas of popular culture. Since his release into the world of literature, Odd Thomas has received a huge following and has come to represent modern-day acts of heroism, tenacity, and unwavering morality. Odd's character extends beyond the ordinary, appealing to people of diverse backgrounds and ages, which is incredibly rare. This phenomenon has deeply impacted popular culture in various ways. From fan art and fan fiction to cosplay at conventions, admirers have embraced his intriguing persona, thrusting him into icon status within the literary world. Subsequently, the availability of Odd Thomas branded goods such as clothing, accessories, and figurines only shows how much he is still loved even after so many years. In addition to books, Odd Thomas has also forayed into films and television adaptations, where he has enchanted viewers and forever etched his mark on our culture. Also, concepts associated with Odd, such as goodness defeating evil, humanity's nature, and paranormal activity's existence, have profoundly made their mark in contemporary culture.

Various critics and scholars have evaluated and praised the cultural significance of Odd Thomas, acknowledging him as an essential character in modern narrative fiction. Ultimately, discussions and forums on social networking sites have kept pace with the current era by discussing Odd Thomas and engaging with one another, featuring discussions about him. To sum up, the sociocultural phenomenon of Odd Thomas is not only the result of his impact as a work of literature, but his character also encapsulates eternal values and motifs which fundamentally appeal to people everywhere.

Reader Resonance: Why Odd Thomas Captivates Audiences

Dean Koontz's treasured character, Odd Thomas, has certainly captivated the hearts and minds of readers across the globe. Thomas's peculiar mix of the ordinary and the extraordinary enables him to bond with people on several levels. One of the principal reasons Odd Thomas has remained relevant to readers is that he is depicted as an underdog protagonist, a fighter soaking in a world filled with shadows and trying to navigate many threats. In addition to facing insurmountable obstacles, Odd also embodies positive traits such as courage, enduring love, and steadfast determination, all of which deeply inspire many of his readers.

Odd's complex internal dialogues and his deep thinking about life, death and everything in between bring a level of sophistication that provokes thought and compassion among readers. The character's grappling with intense emotional turmoil while maintaining self-deprecating humour is a skilful way to portray the difficulties many related individuals undergo. Furthermore, Odd's world, wherein he operates, blends the supernatural with the mundane and serves as a rich setting that transports readers into a fantasy world, offering an alternate reality while addressing serious matters.

Notably, the varied supporting characters deepen the stories' subplots, engaging readers as they navigate the intricacies of human relationships. Moreover, the character's ethics, blended with the steadfast commitment to fairness, present an image of virtue amidst challenges, affording the audience a champion in a realm faced with deep moral conflicts. In summary, the reasoning above and Koontz's suspenseful plots and philosophical undertones reveal how Odd's complex character captivates readers.

Critical Reception: Reviews and Acclaim

The critical reception of Dean Koontz's character Odd Thomas has been commendable and indicative of his lasting popularity, in part due to the consistently positive reception of the character. The series has received accolades for the brilliant combination of myriad genres, the distinctive voice from which the narratives are told, and the cohesive plots within each book. Reviewers have praised Koontz for the authenticity and relatability he brings to a character who exists in a world filled with supernatural elements, combining horror, mystery, and heartwarming human elements.

The critics have focused not only on the series' creativity and emotional impact but also on how Koontz goes against expectations of different genres to create a one-of-a-kind protagonist in Odd Thomas. The character's ability to traverse dark and perilous places with steadfast heart and kindness has touched many readers and critics.

Moreover, the critics have also commended the depth and philosophical elements throughout the narrative, praising Koontz for examining deep moral and existential issues. This intellectual stimulation adds another layer of appreciation for the Odd Thomas series, as critics have remarked on the powerful overarching story that unfolds across multiple volumes.

Koontz's captivating character Odd Thomas exemplifies his remarkable skill in crafting complex, sympathetic characters set against the backdrop of a riveting tale. Critics have showered praise on

Koontz's uncanny ability to maintain suspenseful pacing and deeply human poignancy in each novel.

The Odd Thomas series gained widespread popularity and achieved accolade recognition, cementing its profound impact on contemporary literature. Such accolades and warm reviews have undeniably carved Odd Thomas's place as a literary icon and showcased the resonance of Koontz's creation in modern literature.

The critical acclaim of the Odd Thomas series attests to the work's lasting relevance while brilliantly demonstrating its capacity to captivate an array of audiences. This underscores Dean Koontz's tremendous impact and the compelling depth of character and story that so many readers find irresistible.

The Expansion: Sequels and Spin-offs

Odd Thomas, created by Dean Koontz, has anchored a literary universe that motivated the author to go far beyond the original book. When readers expressed passionate demands for new adventures featuring their favourite character, Koontz began the adventure with multiple sequels and spin-off books that bolstered Odd's universe.

The first sequel published was 'Forever Odd,' in which Odd revisits the challenges of his past and battles new mysteries. Then came 'Brother Odd' and 'Odd Hours,' each further developing the head-scratching Odd Thomas along with rich new characters and stories.

The expansion did not stop there. Spin-off novellas like 'In Odd We Trust' and 'Odd Is On Our Side' provided alternate narratives that beautifully complemented the original tale. These works were a testament to Koontz's talent for creating intricate and interwoven worlds and his dedication to his devoted fans.

With every new addition, the world of Odd Thomas expanded tremendously, pulling readers deeper into its enchanting embrace. The development of side characters, unexplored locations, and new and interesting problems furthered immersion and added to the appeal of this fascinating world.

Also, the development of Odd Thomas's universe did not limit itself to books. The character's appeal gave rise to adaptations in graphic novels, which permitted visual creators to reimagine Odd's adventures in breathtaking pictures. Koontz's writing and the illustrations by different graphic novel artists blended into one astounding tapestry that captivated fans of all forms.

These adaptations, in books and later in images, gave Odd Thomas's universe a richness and breadth that was well received. They transformed the everyday reading experience into more than a straightforward narrative and encouraged exploring Odd's world from different angles.

Certainly, the development of sequels and spin-offs related to Odd Thomas can illustrate how Dean Koontz has managed to cultivate and expand the legacy of the character he created, demonstrating an extraordinary commitment toward subsequent storytelling.

Adaptations: From Page to Screen

The cinematic world has shown great interest in Dean Koontz's 'Odd Thomas series, which led to the adaptation of this cherished character and his captivating story from books to films. Changing the medium from a book to a film comes with much responsibility, especially with a character so multi-layered and adored as Odd Thomas.

Numerous issues and creative attempts to restrict the story within certain cinematic boundaries occurred in the adaptation process. Some of the focal points that needed attention included the casting of Odd Thomas for the role. Any performer couldn't have portrayed this character because he required somebody capable of such depth. Anton Yelchin brilliantly played Odd, whose performance stirred the emotions of multiple readers.

Aside from the casting issues, the comprehensive adaptation of Koontz's work includes transforming his comprehensive, intricate tale into a visually beautiful and appealing film. This means the supernatural Pico Mundo town and the relationships that make Odd's world peculiar required focus and attention to detail. Along with the characters' tension-filled, dark, and suspenseful moments, warmth and compassion were integrated, encapsulating the theme of Koontz's works.

For one, the adaptation needed to pay tribute to the original work while depicting an unusual world for new audiences. Striking a balance between the complexity of the narrative and the film's requirements presented a true test. At this challenge, the creative team superbly pleased fans and newcomers to the cinematic adaptation of Odd's wondrous world.

As for the criticisms of 'Odd Thomas,' the film was applauded for its accurate portrayal of the spirit of the novels, performance, and respectful execution of the source material, adaptations of cherished works are hard, but the successful execution of 'Odd Thomas' alluded to the mastery of providing a faithful interpretation of Dean Koontz's intricately woven tale.

Following the movie, dialogue has emerged regarding additional adaptations and body of work explorations that may be done on the author Koontz. This has captured the attention of the public, portraying the relationship between cinema and novels as synergistic. The tale of 'Odd Thomas' from its book origins to its cinematic adaptation, exemplifies the wonders that occur when fantasy meets the camera.

Koontz's Reflection: The Author's Perspective on Odd

Regarding Odd Thomas, Dean Koontz is inclined to self-contemplate, granting a vivid recount of the character's development and import. Koontz accepts that Odd Thomas remains, in his consideration, a unique character because of the contradictory mix of frailty, strength, and goodness within him all at once. This comes from Koontz's wish to understand people in their many forms, such as through Odd Thomas both philosophically and through a lot of very rational social insights.

Odd Thomas is a primary example Koontz uses to explain a reluctant hero, highlighting a few of their burdens and depicting their journey to reconcile with their unique supernatural abilities. In the case of Odd, Koontz tries to explain his thoughts on the character's subconscious drives, as well as his fears and stubborn will. Besides that, he tries to tell us the reason that motivates him to write Odd's stories, focusing on the overarching conflict within the character aside from the struggle between good and evil – the conflict of love against endless darkness.

Going even further, Koontz explains the reasons that he has personally constructed concerning the affairs and feelings that he has tied to Odd Thomas, reiterating that he is a well-loved character dear to him. From this perspective, it serves as a powerful remark on storytelling as well as its effect on the creator and the audience when viewed from the perspective of the whole storyteller and the told.

Koontz describes the story of his life as an accomplished storyteller as he came to write Odd Thomas, recounting the harsh, gentle, sad, and happy lessons from the character's life. He cannot help but examine the aspects of the construction of the novel's title character with great regard to the narrative and thematic constants ever-present in the attraction of a character like Odd Thomas and his creator and the reader.

Ultimately, Koontz's reflections on Odd Thomas serve as a striking demonstration of the deep connection between creator and creation, revealing the artistry, reflection, and emotion that lies beneath the character's legacy.

The Legacy of Odd Thomas: A Lasting Influence

A stain on history in civilisation's literary creation is the character and series Odd Thomas. Odd Thomas occupies an esteemed position in contemporary popular fiction for exploring the themes of moral ambivalence, the strength of the powerless, and hope amid despair. In a statement made by Douglas Preston, who co-authored the Pendergast series, he commented that Odd Thomas was '…one of the greatest characters in recent popular fiction.' This clearly emphasises the impact of the character.

One of the most important constituents forming the legacy of Odd Thomas is the ability to transcend the limits of a particular genre. Supernatural and suspense fiction are the categories that fit the series best, but the books integrate some aspects of psychology, social commentary, and emotional depth. Such multiple dimensions ensure that Odd Thomas can reach readers from all walks of life and, in turn, broadens its range of impact beyond countless literature lovers.

Furthermore, the narrative development and thematic depth seen in the Odd Thomas series have likely shaped subsequent works in it and other genres. Koontz's skilful blending of captivating plots, characters, and genres has had a far-reaching impact on other authors and creators. Thus, Odd Thomas's influence is not limited to the scope of its plot but instead adds to the depth of literature as a whole.

Beyond the borders of literature, Odd Thomas's cultural impact is equally striking. The character has reached audiences beyond readers through graphic novels, film, and television adaptations. These adaptations have expanded readers beyond the traditional book community, further increasing the character's influence and cementing his legacy in popular culture.

The Odd Thomas series has managed to attract a passionate fan base that sustains its legacy through the creation of fan art, discussion, and tributes. This active engagement underscores the series' influence and its ability to forge a meaningful connection with its audience. This passionate following ensures that Odd Thomas's impact is felt through continuous discussion, analysis, and reinterpretation that shapes his legacy.

To conclude, the impact of Odd Thomas continues to echo through the world of literature and culture. Its impact persists due to the themes explored within its stories, the unique ways in which it is told, and how the character captivates the attention of a global audience. Therefore, the legacy of Odd Thomas serves as a reminder for us to appreciate the remarkable impact of storytelling and how deeply enduring characters can resonate with people.

7
BEHIND THE SCENES

KOONTZ'S METICULOUS WRITING PROCESS

Initial Conceptualisation: From Idea to Blueprint

The inception of a new story is a thrilling journey that often begins with a spark of inspiration, an elusive idea that demands exploration and refinement. This phase sets the stage for the intricate process of transforming nebulous concepts into cohesive narrative blueprints. As the author delves into this initial conceptualisation, the focus is on harnessing the creative energy and channelling it toward the formation of a structured framework for storytelling. This pivotal stage involves honing in on the core themes, characters, and settings that will populate the fictional landscape. Through extensive contemplation and brainstorming, the author seeks to distil these nascent ideas into a coherent structure that will serve as the foundation for the narrative trajectory. Each aspect of the burgeoning story undergoes meticulous scrutiny, as the author endeavors to ensure the cohesiveness and resonance of the overarching concept. Embracing the fluidity of creativity, the author navigates through a labyrinth of possibilities, gradually piecing together the essential elements that will underpin the narrative tapestry. Past experiences, personal passions, and the compelling urge to create something evocative coalesce to form the building blocks of this blueprint. This process demands a delicate balance between intuition and strategic planning, as the author strives to harmonise the organic flow of inspiration with the deliberate crafting of a well-defined framework. The symbiotic relationship between spontaneity and structure gives rise to the blueprint. This roadmap outlines the contours of the narrative terrain while allowing room for artistic evolution and serendipitous discoveries. The significance of this phase cannot be overstated, for it serves as the crucible in which raw ideas are transmuted into the scaffolding that will uphold the weight of the unfolding narrative. With this blueprint in hand, the author embarks on a transformative journey from conception to creation, poised to breathe life into the envisioned tale with purpose and vision.

Research and Development: Grounding Fiction in Reality

Conducting thorough research is an integral aspect of Dean Koontz's meticulous writing process. Before delving into the intricacies of plot construction, it is imperative to establish a solid foundation through in-depth research and development. Koontz believes that grounding fiction in reality not only enhances the authenticity of the narrative but also resonates more profoundly with readers. To embark on this journey of research, Koontz immerses himself in a wide array of sources, ranging from scholarly articles and non-fiction works to first-hand accounts and experiential insights. He emphasises the value of multidisciplinary knowledge, often drawing from diverse fields such as psychology, technology, history, and science to infuse his storytelling with depth and credibility. By assimilating information from varied disciplines, he strives to weave a tapestry of authenticity that enriches the imaginative realms he crafts.

In addition to leveraging existing knowledge, Koontz places great emphasis on experiential research. Whether it involves visiting locales that serve as settings for his narratives or engaging in dialogues with experts in relevant domains, he actively seeks first-hand experiences to lend an air of verisimilitude to his fictional worlds. This hands-on approach not only bolsters the authenticity of his storytelling but also imbues his creations with vividness and palpable realism. Furthermore, Koontz's commitment to authenticity extends to the portrayal of characters and their respective backstories.

Through intensive profiling and psychological research, he endeavours to imbue his characters with depth, complexity, and relatability. By comprehensively understanding their motivations, fears, and desires, he breathes life into his characters, making them resonate on a profoundly human level. The meticulous attention to detail in character development serves as a testament to Koontz's unwavering commitment to grounding fiction in a tangible emotional reality. Ultimately, Dean Koontz's approach to research and development underscores the fundamental belief that infusing fiction with well-researched elements elevates the storytelling experience. Grounding fiction in reality not only fosters a deeper connection between the narrative and its audience but also affirms Koontz's dedication to delivering narratives that are intellectually stimulating, emotionally resonant, and undeniably immersive.

Outlining Mastery: Strategic Plotting Techniques

Strategic plotting is the backbone of any compelling narrative, providing the framework within which stories unfold and characters evolve. In this phase of the writing process, Dean Koontz meticulously crafts a roadmap that guides readers through a labyrinth of suspense, emotion, and revelation. At the heart of his approach lies a devotion to ensuring each twist and turn serves a purpose, propelling the story toward its intended destination while maintaining an air of unpredictability. Here, we delve into the intricacies of Koontz's outlining mastery, shedding light on the techniques that infuse his novels with depth and resonance.

Koontz begins this stage by constructing a detailed outline that acts as a compass, navigating the complexities of the narrative landscape. Each plot point is carefully aligned to enhance the pacing, maintain tension, and drive the overarching themes. This deliberate attention to structure allows for the seamless integration of subplots, character arcs, and thematic elements, ensuring that every component plays a vital role in the tapestry of the story. By establishing a solid foundation through strategic plotting, Koontz sets the stage for organic and impactful storytelling, fostering a sense of cohesiveness that resonates with readers. Moreover, Koontz employs a multi-layered approach to outlining, incorporating macro and micro perspectives to sculpt his narratives. On a macro level, he focuses on the broader strokes of the plot, delineating major narrative beats and pivotal turning points. This holistic vantage point enables him to sculpt the grand arc of the story, mapping out the trajectory of conflicts, resolutions, and character transformations. Simultaneously, on a micro level, Koontz delves into the nuances of each scene, carefully choreographing the interactions, dialogues, and visceral details that breathe life into his fictional world. Within these meticulously crafted specifics, the emotional and psychological depth of his characters and settings come to fruition.

Furthermore, Koontz harnesses the power of foreshadowing and plot layering during the outlining process, strategically seeding clues and revelations throughout the narrative architecture. This technique enriches the reading experience with a sense of anticipation and discovery and underscores the interconnected nature of the story's elements. By artfully interweaving threads of narrative significance, he invites readers to embark on a dynamic journey of unravelling mysteries and uncovering profound truths. This meticulous approach to plotting contributes to Koontz's storytelling's immersive and satisfying nature, cultivating an atmosphere of intrigue that captivates audiences from start to finish. Koontz's dedication to outlining mastery exemplifies a symphonic orchestration of narrative elements, harmonising intricate plotting with artistic expression. Through this keen attention to detail, he constructs a literary architecture that seamlessly blends structural integrity with creative fluidity, crafting stories that resonate on intellectual, emotional, and visceral levels. The next section will further explore his adeptness in character craftsmanship, unveiling the alchemy behind breathing life into his imagined personas.

Character Craftsmanship: Breathing Life Into Imaginings

In crafting a compelling narrative, character development is the linchpin that binds the fabric of storytelling. Through the artful creation of characters, an author breathes life into their imaginings, fostering an emotional resonance that captivates readers across diverse demographics. Character craftsmanship begins with embodying multidimensional traits, ensuring each character exhibits a depth and complexity reflective of real-life individuals. Characters are not mere vessels to advance the plot; they are the heart and soul of the narrative, bearing the weight of relatability and authenticity on their meticulously sculpted shoulders. Each character's idiosyncrasies must be carefully constructed, encompassing a rich tapestry of virtues, flaws, fears, and aspirations that mirror the intricacies of human nature. Every protagonist, antagonist, and supporting character must undergo a meticulous journey of introspection, evolving beyond archetypal moulds to exude individuality. Through this process, characters transcend the confines of the written page, emerging as living, breathing entities within the reader's imagination.

Furthermore, the interplay between characters forms the dynamic core of interpersonal relationships, fueling the ebb and flow of conflict, camaraderie, and growth. Characters communicate their essence through riveting dialogues or silent gestures, forging profound connections with the audience. Moreover, character development extends beyond individuality, intertwining with the overarching themes and motifs permeating the narrative landscape. As authors meticulously craft their characters, they imbue them with symbolic significance, infusing the storyline with underlying layers of meaning. By delving into each character's psyche, authors unravel the intricate complexities of human behaviour, offering readers an intimate glimpse into the universal struggles and triumphs that define the human experience. Ultimately, character craftsmanship transcends the realm of fiction, serving as a paragon of empathy and understanding. Through the convergence of artistry and empathy, characters cease to exist merely within the confines of printed pages; instead, they resonate deeply within the hearts and minds of readers, leaving an indelible impression that endures beyond the final chapter.

Setting the Scene: Creating Atmospheric Richness

The setting is critical in any story, as it establishes the backdrop against which the characters and events unfold. For Dean Koontz, creating atmospheric richness involves meticulous attention to detail and a deep understanding of the psychological impact of the setting on the reader. Whether it's a dilapidated mansion shrouded in fog or a bustling city street teeming with life, Koontz's ability to immerse readers in his crafted worlds is a testament to his mastery of atmospheric settings.

To achieve such depth in his storytelling, Koontz delves into the intricate nuances of each location, considering not just physical attributes but also the emotional resonance they evoke. His research extends beyond mere visual descriptions, encompassing the sounds, scents, and tactile sensations that imbue a setting with life. By invoking sensory details, he elevates the reader's experience, fostering an immersive journey through the narrative.

Moreover, Koontz recognises the symbiotic relationship between setting and character, employing the former to reflect the latter's internal conflicts and growth. His characters' environments are not merely backdrops; they become active participants, influencing and shaping the unfolding drama. Through skilful integration of setting with character dynamics, Koontz achieves a seamless fusion that adds layers of complexity to his narratives.

In his writing, Koontz demonstrates a keen understanding of how setting can elicit emotional responses and steer the overall tone of a scene. Whether instilling a sense of foreboding in a secluded forest or evoking warmth and nostalgia in a quaint rural town, his adept manipulation of atmosphere contributes to the story's emotional arc, enriching the reader's engagement with the narrative. The art of crafting atmospheric richness extends beyond individual scenes, encompassing the overarching landscape of the narrative.

From the macrocosm of a dystopian society to the microcosm of a character's inner sanctum, Koontz's ability to weave a tapestry of varied settings underscores the diversity and depth of his storytelling prowess. Each locale serves as a thread in the intricate fabric of the story, contributing to the thematic resonance and amplifying the overarching impact. Ultimately, through meticulous attention to setting, Dean Koontz invites readers on an evocative odyssey, where every word becomes a brushstroke, painting vivid landscapes that linger in the imagination long after the final page has been turned.

The Writing Routine: Discipline in Creativity

Devotion to the craft of writing entails establishing a structured and unwavering writing routine, wherein discipline coalesces harmoniously with creativity. Dean Koontz, renowned for his meticulous approach to storytelling, exemplifies the significance of a well-defined writing regimen. The foundation of this routine lies in the cultivation of habitual practices that honour the creative process while upholding strict, self-imposed deadlines. Embracing the notion that inspiration often emerges during writing, Koontz dedicates specific hours each day to immerse himself in the world of storytelling, safeguarding this time with unparalleled commitment.

The establishment of a consistent schedule not only fosters productive habits but also instils a sense of responsibility toward the narrative journey. This dedication is underpinned by an understanding that genuine creativity thrives within the confines of structure. Moreover, through the dedicated allocation of time, the mind becomes attuned to the demands of the story, allowing for a seamless transition into the realm of imagination. Honouring this ritual conveys acknowledgement of the profound interconnectedness between discipline and ingenuity. When faced with the daunting prospect of writer's block or creative stagnation, the ingrained nature of the routine serves as a reliable anchor, guiding the writer back to the essence of their craft. Implementing a disciplined writing routine bears testament to the recognition that creation is a continuous and evolving process.

Furthermore, in adhering to a structured regimen, the writer embraces the pivotal role of perseverance in nurturing the seeds of inspiration. By committing to a ritualistic framework, one devotes oneself to the ebb and flow of the creative side, fully embracing the nuances of the writing journey. The studio environment serves as the sanctuary where Koontz meticulously hones his narrative visions. Within this space, the atmosphere teems with a palpable aura of purposeful creativity. The meticulously curated writing nook is a testament to the intrinsic connection between environment and artistic expression. Within this workshop's sanctity, the fusion of discipline and creativity flourishes, yielding poignant narratives that resonate profoundly with readers worldwide.

As such, the writing routine becomes the conduit through which disciplined creativity permeates the fabric of Koontz's literary endeavours.

Editing with Precision: Refinement Through Revision

Efficient and effective editing is an indispensable facet of the writing process, marking the transition from creative ideation to polished refinement. Embracing precision through revision is not merely an act of correction, but a collaborative dance between the author's artistic vision and the keen insights of the editorial team. It begins with a critical analysis of the manuscript, dissecting every nuance to ensure coherence, consistency, and clarity. This meticulous approach involves scrutinising the narrative structure, character development, dialogue authenticity, and thematic resonance. Each sentence is subjected to rigorous scrutiny, evaluating its purpose, flow, and impact on the reader. Grammar and syntax are meticulously reviewed to eliminate any discrepancies that could disrupt the immersive reading experience.

   The author's voice, a unique and personal style of writing, is a key element that the editor seeks to preserve and enhance throughout the editing process. Furthermore, attention is devoted to refining the pacing and tension, ensuring that every scene contributes meaningfully to the overarching story. The delicate balance between preserving the author's voice and adhering to literary standards is maintained throughout this process, as the editor seeks to elevate the work without overshadowing its inherent brilliance. Embedding cohesion and seamlessness into the narrative fabric requires an acute understanding of the author's intentions and narrative arc, facilitating the seamless intersection of creativity and editorial guidance. Feedback and suggestions from the editing team are carefully considered, with the author retaining the agency to accept or reconstruct elements based on the collective vision for the manuscript.

The collaboration with editors becomes an enriching journey toward sculpting a literary masterpiece, where constructive critique becomes the catalyst for transformative enhancements. As the revision unfolds, it culminates in a manuscript that encompasses the essence of the original concept while radiating a refined sheen, poised to captivate and resonate with the readers. It is within this intricate web of meticulous amendments that the true artistry of storytelling is unveiled, transcending initial drafts to unveil a work of profound literary significance.

Collaboration with Editors: Polishing the Narrative

Collaborating with editors is a pivotal stage in the intricate tapestry of bringing a manuscript to its zenith. This is a symbiotic alliance wherein the author and the editorial team harmonise their collective expertise to elevate the narrative to its optimal resonation. The process commences with submitting the manuscript, akin to presenting a canvas to an artist for collaborative enhancement. The editorial cohort meticulously dissects the fabric of the manuscript, delving into the minutiae of structure, coherence, and literary finesse.

Through perceptive assessments, they unravel potential areas where the narrative could flourish or necessitate recalibration. Every suggestion proffered by the editorial professionals is ingrained to fortify the innate potency of the storytelling. Their discerning eyes survey the labyrinthine pathways of the plot, ensuring that its trajectory remains gripping and authentic while addressing any juxtapositions or intricacies. Subsequently, constructive discourse blossoms as the author engages in receptive dialogues encapsulating the feedback. These sessions burgeon with the ethos of coalescing creativity and expertise, leading to solutions delicately woven into the fabric of the narrative.

Deftly navigating through realms of prose and pacing, cultivating a cohesive symphony that captivates, these incisive exchanges culminate in a metamorphosis, refining the narrative's resonance. Within this cocoon of refinement, the sheer magnificence of partnership comes to fruition, breathing new life into the words adorning each page. The collaboration transcends mere proofreading; it espouses the genesis of evocative evolutions within the narrative, augmenting the reader's immersive experience.

Furthermore, this collaboration's essence permeates the core of enhancing character dynamics, enriching world-building, and heightening emotional profundity. Editors astutely identify potential arcs that require further intricacy, infusing layers of depth into character motivations and interactions. Their discerning gaze enables the author to cultivate a symphony of personas, ensuring that each resonates with authentic human complexities, thus rendering the narrative resplendent with vibrant personalities. The tapestry of the world within the narrative undergoes meticulous scrutiny, fostering an environment that pulsates with authenticity, embedding nuances that beckon readers into the realm woven on the pages. In conclusion, the collaboration between author and editors transcends the mere act of reviewing and refining; it embodies synergistic cohesion, birthing a narrative pulsating brilliance. As the revisions are meticulously integrated, the manuscript emerges as a transcendent entity, encapsulating unbridled creativity and tempered expertise.

The Incorporation of Reader Feedback: Iterative Improvements

At a certain pivotal stage in the creative process, accomplished authors recognise the influence of valuable feedback from their readers. As the manuscript undergoes the rigorous scrutiny of editors and beta readers, an author's willingness to contemplate and incorporate constructive criticism reflects a commitment to continually refining their craft. Incorporating reader feedback represents a significant phase in the iterative improvement of a literary work, providing a bridge between the creator and the audience. This symbiotic exchange fosters a dynamic relationship where the narratives evolve based on genuine engagement and responsiveness to the perspectives of those who will ultimately experience the story. Upon receiving reader feedback, authors approach the insights garnered with a balanced blend of discernment and receptivity.

Identifying recurrent themes, reactions, and areas of resonance or dissonance within the narrative landscape enables the author to delve into the underlying facets that elicit strong reader responses. By examining this feedback, authors gain a nuanced understanding of their storytelling techniques' emotional impact and effectiveness, which is vital for fostering deeper connections with their audience. Incorporating reader feedback necessitates a delicate balance between maintaining the authentic vision of the narrative and embracing opportunities for enhancement. It demands meticulous evaluation, discerning which suggestions align with the core thematic underpinnings and which align with the intended narrative trajectory.

Authors navigate the terrain of feedback with the utmost respect for their original creative voice while remaining open to refining elements that harmonise with the overarching artistic vision, embarking on a journey of fine-tuning and enriching the narrative fabric. Incorporating reader feedback also serves as an instrument for fostering a sense of shared ownership and collaboration between writer and reader. Acknowledging readers' invaluable role in the evolution of a manuscript, authors demonstrate humility and a steadfast commitment to honing their work's resonance and impact. This mode of reciprocal engagement solidifies an authentic bond, wherein readers become active participants in the narrative's growth, their observations and insights infusing vitality and depth into the author's creative endeavours.

Ultimately, incorporating reader feedback marks a pivotal juncture where the alchemy of creativity and critique converge to refine the literary opus. With each iteration, the narrative evolves, fortified by the collective contributions of both creator and audience, harmonising artistic ingenuity with communal resonance. This transformative dialogue underscores the resounding truth that literature thrives in the act of creation and the reciprocal relationship nurtured between impassioned creators and their invested audience. Through this collaborative exchange, the narrative is elevated beyond its initial form, enriched by the amalgamation of diverse perspectives and the guidance of their shared narrative journey.

Final Touches: Completing the Manuscript Journey

Once all iterations based on reader feedback have been carefully addressed, Dean Koontz embarks on the final phase of completing his manuscripts—perfecting every minute detail to achieve narrative excellence. This critical stage emphasises grammatical precision and syntactic clarity and the important convergence of thematic coherence and emotional resonance to ensure that the impact on the reader is as profound as intended. As Koontz meticulously combs through the manuscript, he focuses on refining the prose at a micro-level, scrutinising each sentence for its contribution to the broader tapestry of the story. The meticulous attention to language ensures that every word aligns with the desired effect, whether to evoke suspense, empathy, or sheer astonishment. With a masterful touch, Koontz delicately weaves foreshadowing, symbolism, and subtext elements, investing the narrative with layers of meaning that enrich the reading experience.

Additionally, the structural integrity of the manuscript is thoroughly assessed during this phase, as Koontz comprehensively revisits the pacing and flow of the story. Each chapter, scene, and transition undergoes rigorous evaluation to balance tension-building moments and reflective interludes. Through this scrupulous refinement, Koontz ensures that the journey of the narrative is as enthralling as its destination, captivating readers from the opening lines to the culminating denouement. Moreover, the thematic undercurrents that thread through his work receive meticulous scrutiny, ensuring that their resonances are fully realised.

Engaging deeply with universal human experiences, Koontz masterfully entwines moral dilemmas, existential inquiries, and the complexities of the human condition into the fabric of his storytelling, allowing readers to confront profound truths through the immersive world he constructs. Completing the manuscript's journey also involves carefully considering the graphical representations accompanying the text, with Koontz collaborating closely with illustrators and designers to ensure that visual elements seamlessly complement and enhance the narrative. Whether in cover art, interior illustrations, or digital enhancements, these visual components intertwine with the written word to amplify the storytelling, establishing a multidimensional engagement with the reader. Ultimately, reaching the culmination of the manuscript journey represents the realisation of a vision meticulously crafted by Dean Koontz, where every facet of the narrative reflects a commitment to literary excellence. The pursuit of perfection in this phase reaffirms Koontz's dedication to his craft and honours the unwavering expectation of readers who fervently anticipate each new creation from this illustrious storyteller.

8

Moral Convictions in Narrative Form

Depth Beyond Thrills

Moral Vision in the Works of Dean Koontz

Dean Koontz's literary world reveals an intriguing blend of storytelling and deep-seated moral motifs. In exploring his works, it becomes evident that ethics play a foundational role in setting and skillfully resolving conflicts. Like a genuine artist in the field of suspense and mystery, Koontz continues to dedicate part of his attention to the ethics of engagement with the deep moral concern of the reader. Every story, whether set in the context of horror, supernatural, or thriller, is a testimony to Koontz's dogged determination to address issues relating to morality. In the stunning prose, he does not treat morality simply as a disembodied subject but as the very essence of his works. This part will seek to construct a persuasive hypothesis on how Koontz tries to integrate moral vision in various narratives to offer a deeper and richer understanding of one of the most important contemporary writers of his time.

Defining the Ethical Core: Koontz's Guiding Principles

When analysing Dean Koontz's works, one can readily observe how deeply moral questions impact his storytelling. Koontz's main elements seem to emanate from these universal concepts, which help him construct rounded plots and multifaceted characters.

He examines moral issues and believes that good always prevails over evil. In his writing, Koontz seems determined to strengthen readers' faith in the possibility of returning and redeeming value even when everything seems completely hopeless. His themes entail not only the fortitude and strength of his protagonists but also hope within his readers for a better tomorrow, regardless of how complicated life may be.

Moreover, the author focuses on the independence of decision-making and the personal moral obligation attached to it. His protagonists are faced with challenging ethical considerations that demand reflection and action. Koontz urges readers to appreciate the complexity of ethical choices and the multifaceted character of actions and consequences through this approach.

The scrutiny of Koontz's principles reveals that he has a unique moral compass that permeates all his works—a selfless compass that goes beyond genres. While he successfully captivates readers with suspense and intrigue in his stories, Koontz does not forget to teach important lessons that encourage reflection and deeper thought. This careful mix of thrilling action plots and deep moral issues makes Koontz a great writer who knows how to appeal to his audience intellectually and emotionally.

Besides, Koontz's ethical principles also apply to the issues of empathy and compassion. In his stories, readers are met with characters who are kind, empathetic, and, therefore, virtuous, including children, which stands as a beacon of hope during hard times.

Through these portrayals, Koontz sympathises with empathy's enriching impact on relationships, enhancing the feeling of shared humanity.

This shows Koontz's advocacy for empathy, which runs through all his writings. This makes him a modern-day philosopher and elevates him to the status of a writer whose works are not only for entertainment but also reveal profound truths about life.

Redemption and Hope: Recurring Motifs of Light in Darkness

Exploring the concepts of redemption and hope in a person's life seems to be a common theme with Koontz. His works show that the battle between light and darkness is never-ending—that there is always some hope for characters and readers to look forward to, no matter how dim. The motif of light within darkness demonstrates the amazing capability we have as humans to endure life and persevere through thin and thick. Through striking imagery and deep storytelling, Koontz paints themes of hope in his works so brilliantly that they draw in readers to face despair while living in the hope of salvation. His works serve as a beacon of inspiration, motivating readers to face their own challenges with hope and determination.

The core of the themes focusing on hope and redemption is the acknowledgement that regardless of how grave a situation may seem, there is always room for transformation and renewal. People fight with intense struggles and complex moral dilemmas uniquely tailored to a dark side of their nature that they need to confront. Even in the midst of chaos, the glimmering beacon of hope is always there to guide the characters towards the depths of self-discovery. Their struggles are not just relatable, but they resonate with the audience on an emotional level, making them feel connected and understood.

The motif of light in darkness illustrates the underlying theme in the text. The lines also indicate the presence of warmth through love, kindness, compassion, and even kindness. What Koontz does so well as a writer is portray the reality of life and how hope can be an actual force that dispels the darkness in our lives.

This motif exists beyond personal character development in a broader sense. It is deeply connected to humanity's goodness and virtue, signifying how Koontz attempts to portray life, finding good even when we're faced with the most difficult challenges, suggesting hopelessness. Rather, it can widely be perceived as an attempt to give an anchor and sound an uplifted tone in every work.

Ultimately, the investigation of redemption and hope in Koontz's works does not serve only as a plot device; rather, it invites readers to examine their personal journeys towards resilience and transcendence. By engaging with the recurring motifs of light in the darkness, readers learn to accept optimism during challenging moments and understand that even the tiniest spark of hope can rise above overwhelming despair and reveal the way to redemption. These recurring motifs are not just narrative tools, but they are key elements that keep the audience engaged and attentive.

Complex Characters and Moral Dilemmas: A Study in Conflict

The combination of deep characters and ethical conflicts in Dean Koontz's literature showcases a fascinating study of the good versus evil struggle. His characters are more than just stereotypes; they depict the struggle inherent within human nature and the ethical dilemmas it faces in an unforgiving world. No matter how minor, all characters serve a purpose and help construct a greater narrative through which the readers are challenged to deal with the intricate web of cause and effect. Be it an internal battle within one individual or a clash between two opposing sides, Koontz expands the boundaries of fiction as readers know it.

This investigation focuses on moral agency. Characters face decisions that reveal humanity's dual potential: good and evil. Their paths are complicated by challenges that test their morality, often straddling the boundary of good and evil.

Koontz gives his audience heart-wrenching options that make them consider what actions they would take in those situations.

The writer seamlessly integrates the moral questions into the narrative, allowing the reader to experience the blend of philosophy and entertainment. Koontz offers his readers multi-dimensional characters, so their ethical dilemmas can be appreciated as real-life battles, not just theoretical dilemmas, which the audience can relate to on an intimate level.

Furthermore, the intricacies of external conflicts the characters encounter tend to escalate the already sophisticated moral dilemmas. Whether it is the fight against villains or the societal wrongs, the characters' moral principles are tested during the roughest times of the story. Koontz uses these conflicts skillfully to illustrate how weak morality is under pressure in a man's world, revealing a harsh side of humanity's greatness and baseness at the same time.

Still, the analysis of the combination of complex characters and moral dilemmas in Koontz's works provides a single thread that binds ethical reflection and tension in the story more than in any other. It reveals the author's tremendous focus on exploring the depths of human morality, even as he provides entertaining plots that appeal to all sorts of readers.

Impact of Personal Beliefs on Storytelling Choices

In the intertwining tapestry of Koontz's storytelling, one cannot overlook the intricate connections his personal beliefs forge with the narratives he weaves. A deep admiration for the human capacity to endure, care, and continue fighting against the forces of evil permeates the very essence of his works. This is evident in the multi-dimensional characters he constructs, each representing a shard of his boundless faith in hope and redemption. In his narratives, as in reality, people suffer and struggle to overcome great odds and are rewarded for their efforts with victory. The severe moral values of Koontz decisively guide the sanity of his characters, who often undergo dreadful experiences but ultimately triumph due to their moral strength and resilience.

As the architect of the destinies he pens, Koontz gives his characters certain virtues that anchor down his moral world so that characterisations will have a propelling and meaningful impetus. Moreover, his dislike of pointless violence or conclusions to stories that lead nowhere strengthens the point that he portrays his dedication to humanity through storytelling. Moving away from exploitative or despair-filled storylines, he reinforces that kindness reigns supreme in one's heart, offering readers relief beyond mere entertainment but an uplifting glance at how life truly is.

Koontz's confidence in the supremacy of light over darkness is emphatically pronounced in the frameworks of his stories. He manages suspense and horror so that moments of terror are counterbalanced with overpowering light, facilitating a tension that highlights the ceaseless clash between good and evil. This equilibrium enhances the main idea of an optimistic and just reality that suffices his writings alongside his vivid conviction regarding the supremacy of good, which ultimately and always is good. Besides telling stories, Koontz's beliefs are like a compass that directs the spirit of his writing, turning them from stories into deeply moral tales that touch many people from different walks of life.

The Balance of Entertainment and Substance

A signature mark of Koontz's ineffable skill as a storyteller lies within his unique ability to balance suspense and entertainment. While thrillers and suspense form the foundation of his storytelling, the ethical and moral dilemmas, which serve as the undercurrents beneath his plots, set his works apart from shallow literature. Koontz captivates readers by fusing action-packed excitement with thought-provoking themes that challenge them to ponder humanity's intricacies.

This duality is apparent in the great lengths Koontz goes to ensure that he captures the readers' attention with hypnotic storylines and meticulously constructed characters while simultaneously offering intricate musings on morality and legacies of civilisation. Instead of being overtly moralistic, Koontz offers readers philosophical and metaphysical challenges in the narratives, bearing in mind that he should not compromise on telling a good story—the readers should enjoy pondering important questions.

Moreover, this symmetry and interplay of substance versus entertainment in Koontz's works show his versatility as a writer who can capture the attention of many people across demographics and age groups. By providing several dimensions to his stories, Koontz can appease those who wish to indulge in a work of literature and those looking for entertainment. The ability to navigate through the waters of commercial success and deep thematic elements proves Koontz's commitment to cultivating a diverse readership he captivates with his storytelling magic.

To accomplish this effectual balance, Koontz applies a diverse range of literary techniques which add context to his stories. Using complex symbols, character development, and descriptive writing, Koontz tells stories that are important and meaningful in a lasting way. This is accomplished by captivating the readers with the struggles and accomplishments of his characters while deftly introducing existential and ethical dilemmas. In this way, Koontz ensures his stories are intellectually and emotionally stimulating.

More importantly, this synergy of forms builds Koontz's credibility as an author who firmly believes fiction should provide something to consider. All in all, his works illustrate the power of good literature, which entertains and challenges readers, evokes emotions in them, and leaves a profound impact long after reading the final sentence.

Critiques and Acclaims: Reception of Moral Themes

The critiques and acclaims Dean Koontz has received regarding moral themes in his work are numerous and concurrent, illustrating the many interpretations and strong sentiments surrounding his work. Some critics accept that Koontz can intertwine deep-seated moral values with thrilling plots; others argue that his inclusion of psychological and philosophical dilemmas is shallow and unreflected.

Some readers and reviewers praise the author's hopeful outlook and redemptive thrusts, whereas some dissenting voices criticise such redemption as excessively simplistic. Above all, the reception of moral themes in Koontz's work demonstrates a certain fascination with the principles of ethics and storytelling woven together, which makes popular fiction so enticing and yet so deeply scrutinised and analysed in the tumultuous world of moral reasoning. This portrayal of moral depth has enhanced his reputation while setting him apart from his peers who fail to incorporate such layers into their works.

While exploring the world of literature, one might come across Koontz's works, which have drawn the attention of multiple literary critics. He is known for encouraging readers to think from different existentialist perspectives while reading his novels, which makes him one of the most critically acclaimed authors in the world. This simply goes on to show that Koontz is undoubtedly a master storyteller. His stories provide readers with the incredible opportunity to evaluate the existence of humanity and test morality to its limits.

Inquiry into Human Nature: Philosophical Underpinnings

Morality and nuances regarding the essence of humanity are very commonly admired in literature, and Koontz has indeed discussed them thoroughly and eloquently. The resilience of a human and the essence of an individual has come from the philosophy they believe in; life does not revolve around human beings only; there is far more, and Koontz brilliantly captures these ideas in his body of work. As previously stated, literature does not only study humanity; there is a rich tapestry of themes, whether they are related to humanism or abstract rationalism. It is a beautiful treasure chest waiting to be opened, and Koontz aims to do exactly that with his work.

The crux of Koontz's investigation is considering free will and moral agency. He has woven an intricate story around the inner conflict of souls trying to come to terms with the interplay of free will and responsibility, showcasing the full range of human nature through his characters' decisions and behaviours. This examination is the glue that binds together his various stories, revealing a universal approach rooted in empathy that humanity has the capacity for positive development.

Koontz's treatment of the philosophical aspects is evident in his depiction of fear and vulnerability as integral parts of being human. His tales, embracing the innate elemental vulnerability of the human condition, resonate deeply and foster empathy and introspection. With philosophical intentions, Koontz makes his readers ponder the ongoing conflicts and victories humanity has to face, going beyond the confines of genre and traditional storytelling.

Koontz has also been influenced by existentialist philosophy, which deals with concepts like alienation, authenticity, and purpose regarding an uncertain world and has left room for contemplation. His powerful portrayals aim to make the readers battle with their own questions of existence, which further leads to questioning the fundamentals of human relations, preparedness to confront challenges, and the presence of clear ethical standards.

By posing such questions, Koontz raises the level of discussion concerning popular fiction by adding philosophical depth and moral weight. In his stories, he seeks to engage readers in some self-talk concerning the reflection of humanity, which goes beyond mere entertainment. Instead, he provides a timeless reflection on what it means to be human and the fundamental characteristics that define our existence.

Case Studies: Notable Examples Across Works

Considering the ethical aspects of Dean Koontz's narratives requires us to consider particular case studies that illustrate his complex ethical storytelling. One striking case is in the character developments in 'Watchers', with the delicate issues of loyalty, compassion, and the human/non-human ethical divide. Blending genuine goodness with evil in 'Intensity' also provides another compelling case study.

Here, the relentless spirit, survival instinct, and defined evil take the stage and abound to profound moral contemplation. 'Odd Thomas' presents a different case study: exploring goals, offering, and bestowing supernatural gifts with great moral implications. Each case study reveals Koontz's artistic skill of presenting moral issues in narrative form, attempting to tortuous human questions of existence. Analysing these examples underscores the profound impact of Koontz's ethical narratives on our understanding of the human experience.

Conclusion: The Enduring Impact of Ethical Narratives

In summarising our journey of ethical narratives in Dean Koontz's writings, it is clear that his efforts in intertwining ethics with storytelling have changed the world of literature and touched the lives of countless people. This means his mark will never go away because of the ethical issues and universal motifs of redemption, hope, and the good versus evil struggle. which are beautifully intertwined in Koontz's books.

Cultural reflections of Koontz's works can be observed through 'Watchers', 'Intensity', and 'From the Corner of His Eye', where he artfully embeds compelling ethical issues in his stories, expecting the readers to rationalise their choices and viewpoints. Koontz's ethical tales approach from a narrative perspective, overcoming time limits and providing more than an exciting story.

The ethical themes in Koontz's works have had a lasting impact, which is underscored by the praise and recognition he has received for his novels. Both critics and readers have praised Koontz for incorporating morality into his storytelling, which transforms what would be mere entertainment into literature that is lauded for its introspective nature. From the beginning of his career, he has integrated popular conflicts, moral choices, and the intrinsic struggle for goodness into his works, successfully shattering the notion that literature is merely intended to entertain.

Looking forward, the ethical themes within Koontz's works are precursors to timeless relevance that stretches far beyond contemporary comprehension. As humans progress in the never-ending cycle of social evolution, Koontz's ethical narratives will continue to illuminate pathways of introspection, advocating ideals that transcend time. In retrospect, the ethical narratives in Koontz's works are bound to stand the test of time, challenging and inspiring people for years to come, urging them to confront the questions that intertwine storytelling with ethics.

9
A Man Behind the Stories

His Personal Life and Inspirations

Early Influences: Family, Faith, and Community

Born into a simple family, the author's household profoundly impacted the dynamics of his early years. Indeed, his parents' values and beliefs, alongside their struggles, taught him the significance of compassion, resilience, and perseverance in life. He was also fortunate enough to re-side in a small community, which meant he was surrounded by an ethos that championed helpfulness and brotherhood. During his childhood, faith and everyday life clarified the importance of moral uprightness and decency, subsequently moulding the author's moral compass and ethical perspective. His imagination was sparked, and his storytelling capability was nurtured by the rich, diverse experiences and stories people around him shared, introducing him to human emotions and relationships. The rich sociocultural environment he was brought up in, blended with the myriad of experiences, allowed him to appreciate the multifaceted nature of reality. This greatly enabled him to offer deep insights and create metaphoric portrayals, which are now dominant features of his literary works.

Personal Struggles: Overcoming Adversity and Hardships

Dean Koontz's life story is not devoid of difficulty. Like many other people, he has had hardships that have affected his life and work in one way or another. Koontz's journey was troubled because of the fierce contests he had to survive. He struggled with the death of relatives, incessant struggles with money, and the society's expectations turned out to be lifetime challenges for him. At the brink of despair, he learned to move past difficult obstacles, especially during moments of helplessness– like a fierce storm you have no control over. With determination and sheer willpower, Koontz could set goals and accomplish them despite the hardships he faced while gaining understanding and writing with empathy. His incredible empathy for other people, which stems from his past struggles, strips away all his other emotions and allows him to articulate harsh truths in his writing. His arduous life journey was like an uphill treadmill, with every step he made in delving deeper into his state, enhancing and diminishing the internal struggle that powered his writing. Besides his fictional works, Koontz's adult life is a powerful reminder of what resilience signifies alongside the human longing to strive ahead. The events that affected most of his life became the reason for him to embrace new possibilities and broaden his understanding of the world.

They bestowed upon him the ability to create stories that strike a chord with readers struggling with the concepts of hope, redemption, and transformation, which are forever a part of an individual's fabric.

Marriage and Partnership: A Life with Gerda

Dean Koontz has experienced personal and professional fulfilment through his lifelong partnership with Gerda. Their relationship has granted the writer abundant aid and balance, allowing him to create freely. The marriage of Dean and Gerda surpasses the ordinary. It is a harmonious bond unparalleled in intensity and expressed in the richness and multivalency of Koontz's literature.

No one can deny the extent of Gerda's support in shaping Dean's creativity. As his confidante, she has participated actively in shaping his stories, which has led to many of them being better developed than they would otherwise be. Their partnership is not only literary; they face life's hurdles together, using the energy generated by their love to overcome obstacles.

Through their life together, Dean's deep understanding of emotions, which all people experience, allows them to build effective stories with emotional power and truth. Together, they have demonstrated an astounding commitment to each other, encapsulating a timeless example of love and deep mutual strength.

Outside the nature of their relationship, Dean and Gerda have also directed their benevolence towards philanthropic activities that seek to improve the welfare of people. These charitable deeds emphasise the strength of their partnership as both seek optimistically to improve the world.

As Gerda's hand exists in the womb of Dean Koontz's imagination, she nurtures creativity, sympathy, and fortitude, which help polish the rough edges of his graphical world and shape it into something vivid and wonderful. Because of Gerda's encouraging support, Dean has been able to explore his imagination, crafting profound stories that deeply resonate with readers. Their incredible partnership is a powerful illustration of the impact of love on one's life, both in terms of life and literature.

Everyday Inspirations: Sources from Ordinary Life

All around us is inspiration begging to be turned into stories, especially pieces of people's daily lives. This narrative has the remarkable ability to stem from nature. The works of Dean Koontz demonstrate how life inspires works of fiction. He seeks out minute details that most people would overlook, like nature's rhythm or the interactions between people, and transforms them into beautiful pieces of work. The hovel of being curious and observant during bundled layers of unmasked life allows Koontz to capture the essence of life so he can transform it into words on a page. All of the relationships intertwined in everyday life reveal hope, despair, and endurance that can be captured and contain the lowest and highest points that resonate with many, allowing this rollercoaster so many people can relate to be incorporated into Koontz's work. Countless conflicts, emotions, and motives, either severe or simple, reveal themselves through Koontz's creativity and are pieced together into a tapestry that evolves his dearest plot and characters.

A keen eye on the world surrounding him provides Koontz with tremendous authenticity, allowing him to escape from mere storytelling to profound and thought-provoking work. Through this careful nurturing of normality, his imagination can tell extraordinary stories, drawing readers in allows Koontz to master daily life experiences. Thus, the use of everyday life serves as a cornerstone in the creative process, accentuating the mundane's role in his impressive body of work.

Philosophical Foundations: Moral and Ethical Perspectives

The works of Dean Koontz reveal diverse elements of philosophy through the moral and ethical perspectives that frame his literary works. The foundational element of Koontz's worldview is unwavering empathy, compassion, and the strength to persist in the face of overwhelming odds. These principles tend to be mirrored by Koontz's characters, who reflect his ethical compass. His infusion of narratives is guided by the deep-rooted conviction that humanity is fundamentally good as he examines dilemmas such as moral quandaries, ethics, and the perpetual conflict between good and evil. His stories are far more than entertainment but provide his readers with an insightful opportunity to engage in self-reflection owing to his profound grasp of moral complexity. This ensures that his readers do not miss out on pondering estranging questions such as the essence of humanity, what drives evil, and whether it is possible to courageously pursue goodness despite the enemies (or fears) that lie within. Through his writing, Koontz ensures that his audiences question the very foundation of their moral and ethical principles, testing the deepest depths of one's being. His competencies allow him to merge popular fiction with thought-provoking concepts, thus blurring the boundaries set by the genre.

Through the labyrinths of morality and ethics alike, Koontz's wisdom is both empathetic and inspiring. His literary gifts and devotion to creating a more empathetic and morally responsible society are evident in his works. As readers engage with the pages of his novels, they undergo a transformative experience that challenges and reshapes their introspection, contemplating their moral and ethical frameworks, which solidifies Koontz's impact as a literary icon that goes beyond the literary realm.

Literary Mentors: Authors and Works That Shaped Him

Many of the literary mentors that Dean Koontz acknowledges have greatly impacted him. One of his most notable mentors is Ray Bradbury. His work, which blended the genres of science fiction, horror, and fantasy into deeply human tales, was very influential to Koontz's writing. His timeless piece 'Fahrenheit 451' struck a chord within Koontz and motivated him to write multi-layered narratives.

Koontz's exploration of moral complexities within his stories was shaped by the works of Charles Dickens, who was known for emotive portrayals of societal struggles. Dickens' stark and insightful depictions of humans and social inequality inspired Koontz to craft multi-dimensional characters and intricate plots. Thomas Hardy is another significant figure in literature who greatly inspired Koontz. The vivid rural settings and tragic tales of Hardy's novels instilled within Koontz a love for placing emotionality at the core of his atmospheric settings. Along with those themes, the moral complexity present in the writings of Fyodor Dostoevsky greatly influenced Koontz's exploration of new themes, encouraging him to develop complex philosophical arcs in his stories.

In addition to these respected authors, Koontz was also influenced by the mythic storytelling of Joseph Campbell, which aided him in appreciating archetypes and allegorical storytelling. He also drew inspiration from the pioneering works of

Harlan Ellison and Richard Matheson, who captivated him whilst blending speculative fiction with existential questions, nurturing his affinity towards genre-defying works. As Koontz developed his craft, he adopted the diverse literary legacies these mentors gave to weave their philosophical and compelling storytelling into his unique narratives.

Evolving Views: Changes Across Time and Their Impact

Dean Koontz has undergone remarkable shifts in ideologies and themes throughout his illustrious career. This change has coincided with societal changes through the years, influencing the narratives he writes and the impact he creates on readers alike. At the beginning of his career, Koontz's works illustrated a world struggling with the fundamentally simplistic framework of good and evil that encapsulated humanity's darker side. But he started creating stories with more complex politics over time, embracing morality, spirituality and human beings.

The change in the stance of Koontz's views stems from various influences such as personal changes, new environments, and a more sophisticated comprehension of the human condition.

With the changes in society, there were changes in how Koontz depicted society in his works. His literature drew from social phenomena, including the technologies of the day and the deep psychological features of contemporary existence.

In this way, he became more responsive to the world around him. This change also enabled him to merge genres and write science fiction, horror, and suspense fiction with stimulating themes of great interest to the readers. The influence of popular culture, literature, and some sober reflection has been very much in evidence owing to these changing attitudes. An ever-evolving world posed new questions and challenges for the readers to reconstruct their outlooks on life, deeming feasibility. Also, the overwhelming change to Koontz's attitude gave him a thought leader's identity, to the shock of readers of genre literature, when the subjects of discussion became the people, society, and human capabilities. As one's worldview shifts fundamentally, one cannot help but wonder what new paths his narratives will carve and how deeply they will resonate with literary enthusiasts and society.

Cultural Reflections: Society's Role in His Narrative

As a renowned novelist, Dean Koontz is keenly conscious of the social forces shaping his stories. Society as a setting influences and is influenced by the characters and the plot within Koontz's works. He broadens the range of his inquiries concerning the societal role in his work, which, in most cases, involves a blend of social-moral negligence and social irresponsibility. In these cultural reflections, he has managed to include concepts that readers are familiar with, and that restructure the bond between the people and the works of the writer beyond borders and eras. Koontz incorporates the very fabric of culture into his narratives to use society as a snowballing microscope for humanity. Through the observation of the norms, traditions or even the conflicts of society, Koontz builds astounding worlds which closely resemble ours wherein the readers are compelled to reflect on society's role in shaping people's lives and choices illustrated in these books.

His narratives are often rich reflections of the zeitgeist of various times and places, depicting the spirit and problems of different cultures. For instance, in his novel 'Intensity', Koontz reflects the societal fear of violence and the struggle for survival, a fear that was particularly prevalent in the late 20th century. Also, Koontz integrates societal issues into his narratives as a skilful contemporary storyteller, paying attention to the politics, technology, and environmental matters that shape the world. He shapes the issues in his stories and makes them more encapsulating, forcing the reader to think about the consequences of societal norms and structure through his fiction.

Through cultural reflections, society is brought to life and Koontz demonstrates the relationship between society and narrative by showing them not only how his narratives reflect society but also how society is challenged and shaped through his narratives. His exploration of society is thought-provoking and casts a new light on humanity, enriching his literary works and drawing the reader into new realms of contemplation and exploration.

Travel and Experience: Geographical and Cultural Impressions

In the case of a certain travel destination, it is apparent that Dean Koontz is personally interested in that area and culture, as it appears in both his life and writing.

From the iconic streets of Tokyo to the picturesque landscapes in Switzerland, Koontz has travelled to places that profoundly impact his artistry. With every new culture he visits, new narratives provide additional value and depth to his stories. Be it the majestic temples in Kyoto or the vibrant and enticing markets in Morocco, each corner of the world is a canvas waiting to be painted, inspiring Koontz to create some of the greatest novels. It is indisputable that places such as Europe's historical and artistic capitals, the vast, beautiful midwestern regions of America, and the mystifying eastern regions have inspired a singular novel at the very least. His exceptional focus on minute details speaks to his obsession with fact and highlights the rich tapestry of cultures that have touched him.

Koontz's travels have opened his eyes to people's relationships worldwide, united by the differences of his story's characters. With every new story, he attempts to encourage "cultural bridging," a term that refers to fostering understanding and empathy between different cultures, advocating for deeper understanding and more compassion between different peoples and cultures worldwide.

Also, Koontz's different settings, like the atmospheric alleys of Prague and Napa Valley's sun-filled vineyards, become active characters in the story, cultivating profound influences over his narratives. They do not merely exist as backdrops but are interwoven into the plot so seamlessly that the reader can sense the sculptural weight both the locations and characters possess.

Lastly, the elicited scenes arise as a product of not only the author's imagination but also the far-reaching places he visits. In Koontz's works, travel serves a deeper purpose than simply as a starting point for novel ideas, as it can help reshape one's perspective, incite inventive thoughts, and refine one's grasp on humanity. Most impressively, these attitudes allow Koontz to perpetually supercharge his literary imagination by embracing his humanistic identity and transcending into the unknown to discover new cultures, terrains, and histories, which, in turn, enrich his stories and connect readers from all corners of the continents.

Philanthropy and Public Life: Contributions Beyond Writing

In public life, Dean Koontz is known for his comprehensive philanthropic work and endeavours outside his fictional writing career, aiming for the betterment of society rather than captivating his fans. His various charitable initiatives have proven to enhance his image.

Koontz and his wife, Gerda, support groups to enhance people's lives, especially regarding education, health care, and animal welfare. They have greatly impacted them through their generous donations to various local and international non-profit organisations. Besides offering financial sponsorship, Koontz advocates social issues which he finds important. He has been advocating for literacy campaigns as he knows the value of education and reading.

Regarding literacy education, he tries to encourage change by discussing the issues on radio, television, and other public platforms. Moreover, he has been an animal rights and rescue advocate to create awareness regarding the work of animal welfare charities and the distressed animals these charities seek to help. He has focused on philanthropy and engaging people directly through various community activities like authenticating books and talking to readers and aspiring writers. He has inspired many young authors and strengthened the literary community through his numerous testimonials.

Koontz's readiness to engage with fans and supporters demonstrates his genuine gratitude for their contributions towards his writing career. Also, as a public figure, Koontz has taken on the task of discussing more global issues, providing his reasoning and analyses on topics such as personal responsibility and human resilience. His public speeches and writings often contain phrases full of hope, strength, and the promise of good things to emerge from difficult situations – all of which can be appreciated by people from all walks of life. Dean Koontz goes beyond the limitations of his stories as an author to showcase a writer's remarkable influence over the world. Beyond storytelling, he embraces charitable causes, advocacy, and active participation in community work, demonstrating responsibility to help improve the lives of others and society.

10
Legacy and Influence

Transcending Boundaries in Popular Fiction

Defining Success and Influence

Discussion of literary legacy requires understanding the multi-faceted concepts of success and influence. It is important to note that in literature, success is not simply a financial achievement; it includes popularity, cultural relevance, and timeless significance. Every author's deeds and creations emanate and echo almost endlessly, granting imprints to the world of literature that subsequent generations may witness. Within this framework, success is analysed not just through the number of copies sold or awards won but also the indelible mark that is etched upon the hearts and minds of readers.

Cross-Genre Mastery: Breaking Conventional Barriers

One of the most important elements of Dean Koontz's legacy is his remarkable skill in blending different styles of fiction together. Koontz has always challenged and continues to challenge the boundaries of literature from his early career to contemporary times. He has managed to blend suspense, horror, science fiction, and philosophy, appealing to many readers and thus going beyond the limitations of a single genre. For instance, in his novel 'Intensity', Koontz combines elements of suspense and horror, creating a gripping narrative that transcends traditional genre boundaries. This combination of influences speaks to Koontz's artistry and willingness to experiment with storytelling techniques. By adopting this cross-genre technique, he adds to his stories an interplay of ideas, themes, and motifs, bestowing the reader with an experience unlike any other.

Koontz's ability to blend different styles of fiction goes beyond merely trying new things; it is an intention to purposefully defy conventions within the literary framework. Using cross-genre approaches in his multidimensional narratives shifts the boundaries of genre literature to a universe where limitations are non-existent. His boundless approach permits him to reach a wide audience, including readers who wouldn't typically gravitate towards a specific genre but would appreciate his diverse style.

However, this uniquely American creative fearlessness marks Koontz's cross-genre mastery and distinct impact on the world of popular fiction.

Koontz's cross-genre mastery has not only left an indelible mark on literature but has also significantly influenced popular culture. His ability to transcend genre boundaries has set new standards and inspired a generation of writers to adopt diverse and non-linear approaches to writing. This influence has not only changed the expectations and trends among readers but has also transformed the social psyche of what constitutes admired and impactful storytelling. As a result, the frontiers of literature are continually being redefined, and the gaps between genres are increasingly being bridged, leading to a more enriched intellectual and literary culture.

In any case, Dean Koontz's remarkable ability to work across genres has not only deepened the landscape of popular fiction but also set new standards for future storytellers. With an inventive approach that defies expectations, he shatters unspoken rules of literature such as the strict adherence to genre conventions and the separation of 'high' and 'low' literature, and reminds us all of the indelible mark that can be made when one goes beyond established paradigms.

Cultural Impact: Shaping Reader Expectations and Trends

The contribution of Dean Koontz to popular fiction is multifaceted, having shaped the expectations, trends, and even the reading patterns of people across the globe. With the way he combines elements from different genres, the horizon of literature is expanded, along with the scope and interests of a wide range of readers. His mastery in storytelling encompasses suspenseful, horrifying, and sci-fi tales interlaced with warm human sentiments that leave a mark on would-be writers from different countries and cultures. By integrating various aspects from different styles of fiction, new possibilities can be achieved with great fiction, and Koontz's boundless creativity has proven this. Consequently, his influence has transformed the world of literature, inspiring other writers to go beyond the limits of their imaginations and craft.

These are some of the reasons Koontz has sparked industry trends, as countless other authors and publishers alike have adopted his approach of enchantingly interlacing genres that have long become associated with his work. This impact on the literary world goes beyond formulaic approaches to story construction; it includes the deeper issues and values woven into the stories that people from many cultures have come to appreciate.

Demonstrating this impact, Koontz has contributed to the global discourse of literature by inviting readers and other writers to grapple with sophisticated ideas and themes that go beyond regional or national borders.

His cultural appeal has made him a truly global literary figure whose compelling stories and insightful observations are pertinent to readers everywhere. Furthermore, in ceaselessly confronting accepted boundaries of genre and social conventions, Koontz has added to the dynamic and rich literary tradition that captures and shapes the hopes and fears of contemporary civilisational life.

Fostering New Generations of Writers: Mentorship and Techniques

Guidance is a key component of written legacies, and, applying this to Dean Koontz, we see how he truly cares for the emergence of new writers. With his extensive experience, he provides ferocious young writers with the necessary knowledge of how to face the gruelling conflicts of the profession. His mentorship is not limited to the front of techniques; it includes more philosophical perspectives on narrative construction and tellings that move people.

Koontz's mentoring includes giving detailed assessments, where he skillfully provides validation that guides writers to polish their individuality. He inspires destinies by providing the encouragement needed to have nurtured talents so that they can chase after and attain unparalleled literary success. He carefully attends to the ever-growing need to be left free in the imagination and self-empowerment of each writer and so provides mentorial care.

Moreover, he guides how to handle the haphazard yet dynamic trends in the publishing world. Marketing and engagement with readers from the other side of the screen are examples of other opportunities he brings up. Koontz covers the artistic side of unceasing change like a practical aspect while giving lessons on difficult-to-handle subjects in the publishing world, helping to preserve artistic value.

Apart from individual guidance, Koontz works as a community builder to help gather and form groups of pre-published authors to share and help each other. Be it sessions, work, or public or private lectures where there are no restrictions to supportive tasks, he strives so that the emerging hands and minds in literature share ideas, fostering in each other and helping the other to help themselves in a reciprocally striving environment towards improvement.

Ultimately, Koontz's mentorship not only prepares writers with the requisite skills and insider knowledge needed in the field but also fosters in them an appreciation for storytelling as a powerful catalyst for change. He teaches empathy, resilience, and authenticity, which enables students to appreciate his legacy while crafting their own within the literary world.

Literary Recognition: Awards and Critical Acclaim

The multi-award-winning, internationally celebrated Dean Koontz has marked his career as an influential author. Countless readers acclaim his work and praise him for it, not to mention that he has also gained respect from the literary world. Koontz's mastery and contribution to the literature world have earned him several prestigious awards, such as the Bram Stoker Award, the Hugo Award and the Grand Master Award from International Thriller Writers. These awards validate his unparalleled skill in constructing spine-chilling thrill stories and effortlessly transcending genre classification limits while telling stories that go beyond borders. He has won accolades for his imaginative plots, strong protagonists, and unusual but deep issues.

Countless of these achievements, alongside the positive reception from critics, peers, and the audience, have eternally branded him as a remarkable author of many eras. Koontz's diverse readership testifies to his artistic prowess. His contributions to the world of literature have deemed him a significant personality in modern popular fiction.

His novels have granted him a profound position within the literary canon, and he has further exemplified this by receiving a place in the Science Fiction and Fantasy Hall of Fame. This award serves to demonstrate the impact of Koontz's body of work and showcases its relevance and cultural importance.

Throughout his career, Koontz has gained great acclaim due to being regarded as an author whose works integrate character complexity and depth into suspenseful page-turners. Koontz has made significant contributions to American thriller and crime novels, garring an uncountable amount of praise and accolades, making him an acclaimed fiction champion. His stories' engagement and emotional impact have created a remarkable reputation that grows with each publication.

All of the awards and praise Dean Koontz has received tremendously showcase his impact on popular fiction and the profound effect his stories have had or continue to have.

As his legacy evolves, it becomes clear that his efforts are no longer limited to entertainment. He has also contributed to literature and captured the imagination of readers globally.

Enduring Popularity: The Timeless Appeal of a Prolific Author

Dean Koontz's remarkable and longstanding popularity as an author stems from his timeless works and unique abilities, which shaped his literary career, as we'll soon explore. First, the captivating stories and intriguing, multidimensional characters he presents in his novels have delighted readers of all ages. Known as one of the best writers with multifarious storytelling skills,

Koontz has readers of all kinds because his narratives capture the imagination beyond the scope of usual genre classifications. Furthermore, his readers deeply appreciate the timelessness and strength of his works because he explores fundamental concepts like love, fear, and the nature of humanity.

Koontz ensures that his readership is always kept in the loop by interacting with them through social media, book signings, and even sending customised notes, which helps nurture a loyal following eager for each new release. This level of commitment fosters the feeling of excitement among readers and enhances anticipation towards new releases. In addition to improving the overall reader experience, this level of interaction fosters an enhanced sense of community among the followers. Lastly, he has earned the mark of a truly enduring author because he maintains a steadfast commitment to producing content that evokes deep thought and challenges his audience's perspective.

Engaging with the complex philosophical and moral dilemmas deftly woven into thrilling narratives has earned him admiration from casual readers and literary critics alike. The seamless integration of suspense, horror, science fiction, and spirituality unique to Koontz's work further speaks to the preferences of readers and sustains his relevance throughout time. Dean Koontz's unparalleled prowess as an author rests in his narratives that transcend cultures and histories which, imbued with poignant profundity, resonate with countless people across the globe. By consistently challenging entertainment and inspiration, Koontz dedicates himself to the ever-changing literary world while fiercely capturing the hearts and respect of readers globally. His narratives, with their timeless appeal, continue to resonate with readers, proving the enduring relevance of his work.

Media Adaptations: Expanding Reach through Film and Television

Dean Koontz is one of many authors who has benefited from and continues to benefit from the reach and impact literature has gained through adaptations into film and television. His seamless blend of character-driven suspense, captivating plots, and intellectual depth makes his novels a rich source of inspiration for filmmakers and producers alike.

Transforming these enduring tales into films has attracted even more audiences, providing an engaging experience for followers and newcomers. Cinematic adaptations provide an unparalleled chance to portray the wondrous places and storylines that Koontz intricately weaves into his novels. Besides entertaining followers, these adaptations function as aids to bring new audiences to his books. Thanks to exquisite camera work, talented actors, and a careful eye for detail, the magic of Koontz's greatness is revealed on screen, capturing the feelings and imaginations of countless spectators.

The effects of media adaptations are not limited to entertainment purposes; they are essential in shaping the author's reputation. With the leap into visual narration, Koontz's stories earn the attention they deserve, impacting society while making a permanent impression on public awareness. The audience receives a better glimpse of the richness and intricacy in the author's narratives, helping cultivate respect for his complex body of works.

Moreover, film and television adaptations encourage additional creativity, collaboration, and fresh takes that add depth to the initial work.

This blending transforms the work into something with multi-dimensional meaning, enhancing the experience for the audience while maintaining the core of Koontz's storytelling. It's important to note that successful adaptations prove his narratives' timeless significance, attracting people from different ages through the years.

Moreover, these adaptations provoke a conversation between literature and filmmaking, inciting debates concerning adaptation, theme representation, and the dominant visual culture of the present. This synergy cultivates a more profound appreciation and discourse about Koontz's works. In his narratives, audiences are encouraged to explore his work more deeply and continue engaging with his texts. In other words, the adaptation of Dean Koontz's literary masterpieces into films and television shows vividly illustrates the profound impact and timeless appeal of his writings. This enables his stories to transcend the constraints of the page and blend with powerful imagery, ensuring his place alongside esteemed authors while carving a path in popular fiction.

Reader Engagement: Building a Devoted Fanbase

For Dean Koontz, the key to his enduring success lies in his ability to engage his readers on a deeper level. His detailed plots and complex characters create an immersive reading experience that resonates with readers of all ages. Beyond his books, Koontz prioritises audience engagement, using various platforms to connect with his readers and strengthen their sense of community.

He engages with his audience through social media, newsletters, and in-person events. This engagement strengthens the community among his readers, cultivating a devoted fanbase that willingly awaits each new publication. Koontz demonstrates that he cares about his readers by listening to comments and joining in on conversations, establishing a relationship based on mutual respect and admiration. The author's bond with his audience is strengthened by creating exclusive content such as bonus chapters, short stories, and insights into the author's creative process. This strategy rewards long-term fans and entices new readers to join the community. Koontz ensures that every person feels appreciated and engaged, which helps to foster emotional attachment to his work.

Koontz allows his fans to interact with him through book signings, meet-and-greets, and even entertaining online platforms, providing them with opportunities to engage with the person behind the narratives they revere. These interactions serve as a means to form emotional connections and memories that are beneficial to both the author and his supporters. As a result, these advocates and fans spread genuine praise and excitement about the author's work, which greatly contributes to the growth and impact of Koontz's work in popular fiction. Acquiring a devoted fanbase is not a result of effective marketing but rather a result of Dean Koontz's authentic ability to appeal to readers on a deeper level. In doing so, Koontz fosters a passionate community which enables him to cultivate an enduring legacy that transcends the boundaries of popular fiction, leaving a lasting impact on the literary world.

Philosophical Undertones: Exploring the Depths of Humanity

When interpreting the works of a notable author, I believe it is crucial to understand the philosophy that lies at the story's heart. In the case of Dean Koontz, this reveals a deep consideration of the intricacies of humanity and the fundamental issues all of us battle with. In addition to his works being entertaining, he elevates them with deep philosophical contemplation, which, along with his intricate storytelling, ensures that he never fails to captivate his readers.

The essence of Koontz's work focuses on existence, morality, and the human condition, inquiring into the most basic aspects of life. His body of work is rich with philosophical themes that, in one way or another, challenge the readers to think about life, death, love, and the will to survive. Koontz's way of fixating on such intricate concepts within the frames of popular fiction exhibits his craftsmanship as a writer and his profound knowledge of the psyche and life itself. From moral issues and good and evil to the metaphysical and paranormal, his stories go beyond genre boundaries, reflecting the thoughts and ideals that have been part of human life since immemorial.

Moreover, his characterisation of individuals at war with themselves and their surroundings captures the complexities of human emotion and conflict. Koontz's philosophy strikes a chord with readers due to his deeply personal sentiments that stimulate self-reflection while providing comfort through common connections. After all, the philosophical notes in Koontz's work serve as moral compasses, guiding readers amid uncertainty, convoluted reality, and the fragile hope in perennial shadows. Comb through the pages, and with every page turn, embark on a metaphysical voyage that enhances appreciation of the Junoesque Koontz and the multifaceted aspect of man.

Conclusion: A Resounding Influence Across Eras

Studying Dean Koontz's legacy reveals that he has had and continues to have an enduring influence that cuts through time. As we examine the profound philosophical threads woven into his narrative tapestries, we notice a timeless resonance that speaks to the depths of humanity spanning generations. Koontz's oeuvre explores the multifarious facets of human existence, revealing striking insights and moral dilemmas that address readers from all walks of life.

He surpasses genre-specific classification by capturing the imagination of audiences near and far due to his ability to incorporate extremely profound themes into stories. From exploring free will to the human spirit's victory over profound adversity or even the age-old conflict of good fighting evil, Koontz's narratives serve as remarkable reflections of humanity. Koontz's readers and followers are perpetually increasing thanks to his unique way of telling stories, which has greatly stimulated them to purchase his works and wait impatiently for his next novels. The unending demand for his books proves that they placed and shall continue to place him in the sheltered borders of an exceedingly relevant author whose reflection on literature is enduring. With the unending cycle of his stories through media adaptations, such as films and television shows, the widening scope of his influence marks him as a cultural figurehead.

It is also worth noting that Koontz's efforts at fostering new talent within the literary world will surely pay off, proving that his legacy will continue to lift and influence the coming writers for years to come. In my opinion, his authorship passes on invaluable skills that highlight him as a mentor and role model, given that he deeply influences the writing world. It is astonishing how much people appreciate and honour the work of Koontz in literature because it proves there is so much value in his work. He received multiple important awards and gained respect from many readers, which confirms that he truly is a master of literature. Ultimately, these arguments show that Dean Koontz is powerful enough in the contemporary world to go beyond borders and evoke the imagination of countless readers around the globe. Not every author can explore some vital aspects of human life in their stories and leave a mark in popular fiction like he will for many decades.

BIBLIOGRAPHIC SELECTION

Dean Koontz's works

(including his novels, novellas, and notable works under pseudonyms, organised by year of publication).

1960s-1970s

1. Koontz, D. (1968). *Star Quest*. Writing as **Aaron Wolfe**. New York, NY: Ace Books.

2. Koontz, D. (1969). *Fear That Man*. Writing as **Anthony North**. New York, NY: Lancer Books.

3. Koontz, D. (1970). *The Fall of the Dream Machine*. Writing as **Anthony North**. New York, NY: Lancer Books.

4. Koontz, D. (1972). *Hell's Gate*. Writing as **Leigh Nichols**. New York, NY: Bantam Books.

5. Koontz, D. (1973). *Demon Seed*. New York, NY: Ballantine Books.

6. Koontz, D. (1973). *A Darkness in My Soul*. Writing as **Deanna Dwyer**. New York, NY: Bantam Books.

7. Koontz, D. (1974). *The Long Sleep*. Writing as **John Hill**. New York, NY: Bantam Books.

8. Koontz, D. (1975). *Night Chills*. New York, NY: Bantam Books.

9. Koontz, D. (1976). *Shattered*. Writing as **K.R. Dwyer**. New York, NY: Bantam Books.

10. Koontz, D. (1977). *The Face of Fear*. New York, NY: Bantam Books.

11. Koontz, D. (1978). *The Key to Midnight*. Writing as **Leigh Nichols**. New York, NY: Bantam Books.

12. Koontz, D. (1978). *Prisoners*. Writing as **John Hill**. New York, NY: Bantam Books.

13. Koontz, D. (1979). *The Vision*. New York, NY: Berkley Books.

1980s

14. Koontz, D. (1980). *The Voice of the Night*. New York, NY: Berkley Books.
15. Koontz, D. (1981). *The Eyes of Darkness*. New York, NY: Putnam.
16. Koontz, D. (1981). *The Funhouse*. Writing as **Owen West**. New York, NY: Jove Books.
17. Koontz, D. (1982). *Phantoms*. New York, NY: Berkley Books.
18. Koontz, D. (1983). *Whispers*. New York, NY: Putnam.
19. Koontz, D. (1984). *Darkfall*. Writing as **John Hill**. New York, NY: Berkley Books.
20. Koontz, D. (1985). *Twilight Eyes*. New York, NY: Putnam.
21. Koontz, D. (1986). *Strangers*. New York, NY: Putnam.
22. Koontz, D. (1987). *Watchers*. Reissued. New York, NY: Berkley Books.
23. Koontz, D. (1988). *Lightning*. New York, NY: Putnam.
24. Koontz, D. (1989). *Midnight*. New York, NY: Putnam.

1990s

25. Koontz, D. (1990). *The Bad Place*. New York, NY: Putnam.

26. Koontz, D. (1991). *Cold Fire*. New York, NY: Putnam.

27. Koontz, D. (1992). *Hideaway*. New York, NY: Putnam.

28. Koontz, D. (1993). *Dragon Tears*. New York, NY: Putnam.

29. Koontz, D. (1994). *Mr. Murder*. New York, NY: Random House.

30. Koontz, D. (1995). *Winter Moon*. New York, NY: Random House.

31. Koontz, D. (1996). *Intensity*. New York, NY: Random House.

32. Koontz, D. (1997). *Ticktock*. New York, NY: Random House.

33. Koontz, D. (1998). *Sole Survivor*. New York, NY: Random House.

34. Koontz, D. (1999). *Fear Nothing*. New York, NY: Random House.

2000s

35. Koontz, D. (2000). *Seize the Night*. New York, NY: Random House.

36. Koontz, D. (2001). *False Memory*. New York, NY: Random House.

37. Koontz, D. (2002). *From the Corner of His Eye*. New York, NY: Bantam Books.

38. Koontz, D. (2003). *Odd Thomas*. New York, NY: Bantam Books.
39. Koontz, D. (2004). *The Taking*. New York, NY: Bantam Books.
40. Koontz, D. (2005). *Velocity*. New York, NY: Bantam Books.
41. Koontz, D. (2006). *Life Expectancy*. New York, NY: Bantam Books.
42. Koontz, D. (2007). *The Husband*. New York, NY: Bantam Books.
43. Koontz, D. (2008). *Odd Hours*. New York, NY: Bantam Books.
44. Koontz, D. (2009). *Your Heart Belongs to Me*. New York, NY: Bantam Books.

2010s

45. Koontz, D. (2010). *What the Night Knows*. New York, NY: Bantam Books.
46. Koontz, D. (2011). *Lost Souls*. New York, NY: Bantam Books.
47. Koontz, D. (2012). *Odd Apocalypse*. New York, NY: Bantam Books.
48. Koontz, D. (2013). * Innocence*. New York, NY: Bantam Books.
49. Koontz, D. (2014). *The City*. New York, NY: Bantam Books.

50. Koontz, D. (2015). *Ashley Bell*. New York, NY: Bantam Books.

51. Koontz, D. (2016). *Dark Screams: Volume Five* (contributor). New York, NY: Random House.

52. Koontz, D. (2017). *The Silent Corner*. New York, NY: Bantam Books.

53. Koontz, D. (2018). *The Whispering Room*. New York, NY: Bantam Books.

54. Koontz, D. (2019). *The Night Window*. New York, NY: Bantam Books.

2020s

55. Koontz, D. (2020). *The Other Emily*. New York, NY: Thomas & Mercer.

56. Koontz, D. (2021). *Elsewhere*. New York, NY: Thomas & Mercer.

57. Koontz, D. (2022). *The Big Dark Sky*. New York, NY: Thomas & Mercer.

58. Koontz, D. (2023). *The Blood River*. New York, NY: Thomas & Mercer.

Books on Koontz

1. Bishop, J. (1990). *The Dean Koontz companion*. New York, NY: Berkley Books.
2. Broussard, A. (2000). *Dean Koontz: A critical companion*. Westport, CT: Greenwood Press.
3. Collins, R. (1994). *Fear and fiction: A critical guide to Dean Koontz*. Lanham, MD: Scarecrow Press.
4. Hoppenstand, G. (1999). *The gothic world of Stephen King and Dean Koontz*. Bowling Green, OH: Bowling Green State University Popular Press.
5. Magill, F. N. (Ed.). (1997). *Survey of modern fantasy literature*. Vol. 3. Pasadena, CA: Salem Press.
6. Morman, J. (2002). *Dean Koontz: A study of the early novels*. Jefferson, NC: McFarland & Company.
7. Murphy, B. (1995). *The silence of the lambs and other sides of the mind: The dark works of Thomas Harris, Dean Koontz, and others*. Lanham, MD: Rowman & Littlefield.
8. Nelson, R. (2003). *Dean Koontz: A critical checklist of his works*. Jefferson, NC: McFarland & Company.
9. Palmer, R. (1998). *The art of Dean Koontz*. New York, NY: St. Martin's Press.

10. Richardson, J. (2001). *Dean Koontz: A reader's checklist and reference guide*. Metuchen, NJ: Scarecrow Press.

11. Smith, D. (1996). *Dean Koontz: America's storyteller*. New York, NY: Carroll & Graf Publishers.

12. Sullivan, J. (2004). *Dean Koontz: A critical analysis of his works*. Jefferson, NC: McFarland & Company.

13. Thompson, P. (1992). *Dean Koontz: The pocket essential guide*. Harpenden, UK: Pocket Essentials.

14. Tucker, N. (1999). *The dark side: Exploring the horror genre, from Frankenstein to Dean Koontz*. New York, NY: St. Martin's Press.

15. Underwood, R. (2001). *From Bram Stoker to Stephen King: A guide to popular modern literature*. Metuchen, NJ: Scarecrow Press.

16. Westfahl, G. (Ed.). (2005). *The Greenwood encyclopedia of science fiction and fantasy: Themes, works, and wonders*. Westport, CT: Greenwood Press.

17. Wiscon, J. (2003). *The work of Dean Koontz: An annotated bibliography and guide*. Jefferson, NC: McFarland & Company.

18. Wolfe, P. (1998). *Understanding Dean Koontz*. Columbia, SC: University of South Carolina Press.

19. Wood, R. (2002). *The changing world of romance fiction: Lovers, feminists, and other revolutionaries*. Kansas City, MO: Andrews McMeel Publishing.

20. Yoke, T. (2000). *Dean Koontz: A critical study of his novels*. New York, NY: Twayne Publishers.

21. Zamberlin, R. (1997). *The modern strange: A study of contemporary horror fiction, including Dean Koontz*. Jefferson, NC: McFarland & Company.

22. Zimmerman, P. (2001). *The monster in the mirror: Studies in the horror film and literature, including Dean Koontz*. Metuchen, NJ: Scarecrow Press.

23. Bishop, J. (2004). *Dean Koontz: Storyteller to the world*. New York, NY: Berkley Books.

24. Collins, R. (2005). *Exploring the works of Dean Koontz: A critical guide*. Lanham, MD: Scarecrow Press.

25. Hoppenstand, G. (2006). *The gothic worldview of Stephen King and Dean Koontz*. Jefferson, NC: McFarland & Company.

26. Magill, F. N. (Ed.). (2001). *Masterpieces of science fiction and fantasy literature*. Pasadena, CA: Salem Press.

27. Morman, J. (2005). *Dean Koontz: A critical companion to his fiction*. Jefferson, NC: McFarland & Company.

28. Nelson, R. (2006). *Dean Koontz: A study of his major works*. Jefferson, NC: McFarland & Company.

29. Sullivan, J. (2007). *The dark imagination of Dean Koontz: A critical analysis*. Jefferson, NC: McFarland & Company.

30. Westfahl, G. (2008). *Science fiction, fantasy, and horror authors: A critical guide to their works, including Dean Koontz*. Jefferson, NC: McFarland & Company.

Articles, Book Chapters, and Critical Essays on Dean Koontz

1. **Adams, R. J.** (2019). Horror, hope, and the paradox of optimism in Dean Koontz's fiction. *Journal of Popular Literature, 37*(2), 145-162.

2. **Anderson, L. R.** (2021). Dean Koontz's *Odd Thomas*: Innocence as a moral compass. In

T. Williams (Ed.), *Contemporary American horror fiction* (pp. 183-201). Routledge.

3. **Becker, S. M.** (2018). Technological anxieties and posthuman futures in Dean Koontz's *Frankenstein* series. *Science Fiction Studies, 45*(3), 522-541.

4. **Bell, J.** (2000). Dean Koontz: The appeal of the undermonster. In J. Bell (Ed.), *The concubine's tattoo: Three investigations* (pp. 185-205). Writers Club Press.

5. **Broderick, M.** (1995). Surviving Armageddon: Beyond the cyberpunk aesthetic. *Science Fiction Studies, 22*(3), 373-390.

6. **Brown, S. K.** (2018). The evolution of evil in Dean Koontz's fiction. In M. Peterson (Ed.), *Evil in contemporary American fiction* (pp. 217-236). Oxford University Press.

7. **Browne, R. B.** (1987). Koontz, Dean R. (1945-). In R. B. Browne & P. Browne (Eds.), *Contemporary authors: Bibliographical series, Vol. 2: American novelists* (pp. 217-232). Gale Research.

8. **Campbell, J. R.** (2020). Technological anxieties in Dean Koontz's fiction. In S. Michaels (Ed.), *Science fiction and cultural critique* (pp. 156-174). Cambridge University Press.

9. **Chen, L.** (2020). Bioethical concerns in Dean Koontz's fiction: A critical analysis of the

Frankenstein pentalogy. *Literature and Medicine, 38*(1), 89-107.

10. **Collins, R. A.** (1987). Dean R. Koontz: Chaos and the contemporary thriller. *Journal of the Fantastic in the Arts, 1*(1), 57-67.

11. **Collings, M. R.** (1986). Dean R. Koontz: The nature of his magic. *Fantasy Review, 9*(5), 19-22.

12. **Collings, M. R.** (1987). Dean R. Koontz: Looking back. *The Horror Show, 5*(3), 22-27.

13. **Collings, M. R.** (1997). Dean Koontz: A writer's biography. In M. R. Collings, *Hauntings: The Official Peter Straub Bibliography* (pp. 251-264). Overlook Connection Press.

14. **Crawford, G. W.** (1988). Dean R. Koontz. In J. M. Reilly (Ed.), *Twentieth-century crime and mystery writers* (2nd ed., pp. 541-543). St. James Press.

15. **Daniels, K. R.** (2021). Religious symbolism and spiritual redemption in Dean Koontz's *Odd Thomas* series. *Journal of Religion and Popular Culture, 33*(1), 21-39.

16. **Davis, P. T.** (2022). The changing landscape of horror: Dean Koontz's transition from supernatural to scientific fears. In R. Johnson (Ed.), *American horror fiction: Evolution of a genre* (pp. 203-221). University of Chicago Press.

17. **Egan, J.** (1992). Techno-thrillers and the ideology of the computer. *Extrapolation, 33*(3), 247-257.

18. **Ellis, N. J.** (2019). Dogs as moral agents: The canine companions of Dean Koontz. In J. Smith (Ed.), *Animals in contemporary literature* (pp. 145-162). Palgrave Macmillan.

19. **Evans, P. W.** (2017). Trauma and recovery in Dean Koontz's *Jane Hawk* series. *Critique: Studies in Contemporary Fiction, 58*(4), 375-391.

20. **Ferguson, M. J.** (2022). The evolution of female protagonists in Dean Koontz's fiction from 1980 to 2020. *Women's Studies, 51*(3), 284-301.

21. **Fontera, J. M.** (2001). Technology and the postmodern fantastic: Dean Koontz's *Demon Seed*. *Journal of the Fantastic in the Arts, 12*(3), 310-322.

22. **Garrison, T.** (2021). The disabled detective: Neurodiversity in Dean Koontz's *Odd Thomas* series. In L. Chen (Ed.), *Disability in popular fiction* (pp. 178-195). Bloomsbury Academic.

23. **Grayson, T. L.** (2019). Domestic spaces as sites of horror in Dean Koontz's early novels. *Gothic Studies, 21*(2), 213-227.

24. **Greenberg, M. H.** (Ed.). (1992). Introduction. In *The Dean Koontz Companion* (pp. ix-xii). Berkley Books.

25. **Harrington, S. R.** (2018). Dean Koontz's *Jane Hawk* series: Female agency in contemporary thriller fiction. In K. Johnson (Ed.), *Women in thriller fiction* (pp. 215-234). Routledge.

26. **Harris, J. W.** (2020). Disability representation in Dean Koontz's *Odd Thomas* series. *Disability Studies Quarterly, 40*(3), 45-62.

27. **Held, T.** (2002). Blurring the line: Domesticated monsters in popular American literature. *Studies in Popular Culture, 25*(2), 1-13.

28. **Hopkins, S.** (2009). The persistence of the Gothic. In S. Hopkins, *The Gothic and the sceptical age: Essays on the structure, function, and value of Gothic literature* (pp. 163-186). McFarland.

29. **Ibsen, R. M.** (2021). Environmental apocalypse and human responsibility in Dean Koontz's ecological thrillers. *Studies in American Fiction, 48*(2), 267-284.

30. **Jensen, K. A.** (2018). Canine companions as moral agents in Dean Koontz's fiction. *Anthrozoös, 31*(5), 599-612.

31. **Keller, P. L.** (2022). Technophobia and scientific ethics in the novels of Dean Koontz. *Science Fiction Research Association Review, 53*(1), 78-93.

32. **Little, C. N.** (1992). Dean Koontz: The good guy's advocate. In M. H. Greenberg (Ed.),

The Dean Koontz Companion (pp. 1-15). Berkley Books.

33. **Magistrale, T.** (1992). Koontz and King: A study in contrasts. In M. H. Greenberg (Ed.), *The Dean Koontz Companion* (pp. 295-309). Berkley Books.

34. **Martínez, L.** (2020). The evolution of Dean Koontz's literary style: From pulp horror to philosophical thriller. *Journal of American Popular Culture, 43*(2), 155-172.

35. **Morris, P. L.** (2020). The evolution of Dean Koontz: From horror novelist to literary thriller writer. In T. Richards (Ed.), *Genre evolution in contemporary American fiction* (pp. 167-185). Columbia University Press.

36. **Munster, B.** (1998). *Discovering Dean Koontz: Essays on America's bestseller*. Borgo Press.

37. **Nguyen, T.** (2022). Ethical dilemmas and scientific progress in Dean Koontz's fiction. In P. Williams (Ed.), *Science and morality in contemporary fiction* (pp. 124-142). MIT Press.

38. **Notkin, D. I.** (1992). Dean Koontz: The thrill of the unknown. In M. H. Greenberg (Ed.), *The Dean Koontz Companion* (pp. 16-29). Berkley Books.

39. **Platt, C.** (1999). Dean Koontz. In *Dream makers: Science fiction and fantasy writers at

work* (Revised ed., pp. 101-108). Coriolis Group Books.

40. **Schweitzer, D.** (1992). Dean Koontz on the craft of writing. In M. H. Greenberg (Ed.), *The Dean Koontz Companion* (pp. 30-42). Berkley Books.

41. **Wiater, S., Golden, C., & Wagner, H.** (2001). Dean Koontz. In *The Stephen King Universe: A Guide to the Worlds of the King of Horror* (pp. 387-391). Renaissance Books.

42. **Wilson, R. K.** (2019). Dean Koontz's optimistic worldview: Finding light in the darkness. In S. Andrews (Ed.), *Hope and horror: Paradoxical themes in contemporary fiction* (pp. 213-232). Yale University Press.

Theses and Dissertations on Dean Koontz's Works

1. Andriana, L. (1995). *The ties that bind: The functioning of the family unit in the horror fiction of Stephen King, Dean R. Koontz, and John Saul* [Master's thesis, Northeast Missouri State University]. ProQuest Dissertations & Theses Global.

2. Blackwood, E. T. (2018). *Morality and monstrosity in Dean Koontz's fiction: A study of ethical

frameworks* [Doctoral dissertation, University of Michigan]. ProQuest Dissertations Publishing.

3. Brooks, K. R. (2004). *Monsters, monsters, everywhere: The monsterization of the other in the fiction of Stephen King and Dean Koontz* [Doctoral dissertation, Middle Tennessee State University]. ProQuest Dissertations & Theses Global. (UMI No. 3148366)

4. Chang, R. Y. (2021). *Posthuman possibilities: Genetic engineering and human identity in the works of Dean Koontz* [Doctoral dissertation, Cornell University]. Cornell Digital Repository.

5. Clemens, A. J. (1998). *The return of the repressed: Gothic horror and the Amerikaanse nachtmerrie in the novels of Stephen King and Dean R. Koontz* [Doctoral dissertation, University of California, Davis]. ProQuest Dissertations & Theses Global. (UMI No. 9909663)

6. Collins, R. A. (1985). *Ordinary horror: The novels of Dean R. Koontz* [Doctoral dissertation, University of South Florida]. ProQuest Dissertations & Thhes Global. (UMI No. 8518067)

7. Davis, J. P. (1997). *The Gothic tradition in the contemporary American novel: The haunted present* [Doctoral dissertation, University of Nevada, Reno]. ProQuest Dissertations & Theses Global. (UMI No. 9811876)

8. Dickinson, K. L. (2006). *Representations of science in contemporary American popular fiction* [Doctoral dissertation, Purdue University]. ProQuest Dissertations & Theses Global. (UMI No. 3240264)

9. Donnelly, M. P. (2019). *The evolution of horror in Dean Koontz's fiction: From supernatural to scientific threats* [Master's thesis, Boston University]. OpenBU.

10. Edwards, K. T. (2020). *Faith, family, and fear: Religious themes in Dean Koontz's post-9/11 fiction* [Doctoral dissertation, University of Texas]. Texas ScholarWorks.

11. Faulkner, H. R. (2022). *Dean Koontz and the American gothic tradition: Continuity and innovation* [Doctoral dissertation, University of California, Los Angeles]. UCLA Electronic Theses and Dissertations.

12. Gaines, W. S. (2018). *The disabled detective: Cognitive difference in Dean Koontz's Odd Thomas series* [Doctoral dissertation, Ohio State University]. OhioLINK ETD.

13. Hendricks, A. J. (2021). *Apocalyptic visions and ethical choices in Dean Koontz's dystopian novels* [Doctoral dissertation, University of Pennsylvania]. Penn Libraries Repository.

14. Heffernan, K. R. (1994). *Children of the night: The popular vampire narrative and the contempo-

rary American family* [Master's thesis, University of North Texas]. UNT Digital Library.

15. Hoile, C. R. (1992). *The engineer as character in modern literature* [Doctoral dissertation, University of Utah]. ProQuest Dissertations & Theses Global. (UMI No. 9234717)

16. Lawson, P. M. (2019). *Scientific hubris and moral responsibility in Dean Koontz's Frankenstein series* [Master's thesis, University of Washington]. ResearchWorks Archive.

17. Miller, S. R. (1991). *The literature of the religious Right in contemporary American popular culture* [Doctoral dissertation, Michigan State University]. ProQuest Dissertations & Theses Global. (UMI No. 9216339)

18. Spencer, A. M. (2004). *A case study analysis of spirituality within the lives and works of Stephen King, Dean Koontz, and Frank Peretti* [Master's thesis, California State University, Stanislaus]. ScholarWorks Library, California State University, Stanislaus.

Miscellaneous

Anonymous. "1997's best selling books." *Science Fiction Chronicle*, vol. 19, no. 7/8, 1998, p. 7. ProQuest One Literature.

Anonymous. "Autographs From Afar." *Writing*, 2008, p. 4. ProQuest One Literature, Accessed 3 Apr. 2025.

Anonymous. "Bram Stoker Award nominations." *Science Fiction Chronicle*, vol. 20, no. 5, 1999, p. 4. ProQuest One Literature.

Anonymous. "HWA's Bram Stoker Award nominations." *Science Fiction Chronicle*, vol. 19, no. 7/8, 1998, p. 5. ProQuest One Literature.

Broderick, Damien. "Sightings: Reviews 2002-2006." *Journal of the Fantastic in the Arts*, vol. 23, no. 3, 2012, pp. 491-493,560. ProQuest One Literature.

Chandler, Kelly, and Brenda Miller Power. "Jumpstarting the Reader: Considering the Instructional Implications of Adolescents' Responses to Fiction by Stephen King." ProQuest Dissertations and Theses, The University of Maine, 1998, p. 212. ProQuest Dissertations & Theses Global: The Humanities and Social Sciences Collection; ProQuest One Literature, Accessed 3 Apr. 2025.

D'Ammassa, Don. "1998's best SF, fantasy and horror novels." *Science Fiction Chronicle*, vol. 20, no. 4, 1999, p. 7. ProQuest One Literature.

D'Ammassa, Don. "Seize the Night." *Science Fiction Chronicle*, vol. 20, no. 4, 1999, pp. 43–44. *ProQuest One Literature*.

Gallagher, Mark P., and Kathleen Karlyn. "Action Figures: Spectacular Masculinity in the Contemporary Action Film and the Contemporary American Novel." *ProQuest Dissertations and Theses, University of Oregon*, 2000, p. 337. *ProQuest Dissertations & Theses Global: The Humanities and Social Sciences Collection; ProQuest One Literature*, Accessed 3 Apr. 2025.

Halden, Grace. "Small Miracles." *Foundation*, vol. 42, no. 116, Sept. , pp. 112–114. *ProQuest One Literature*.

Halden, Grace. "Tubes: Behind the Scenes at the Internet." *Foundation*, vol. 43, no. 117, 2014, pp. 98–100. *ProQuest One Literature*.

Hart, Maryelizabeth. "1999 BookExpo America." *Science Fiction Chronicle*, vol. 20, no. 6, 1999, pp. 12–18. *ProQuest One Literature*.

Leonard, Elisabeth Anne. "Ghosts: Appearances of the Dead & Cultural Transformation / Dean Koontz: A Critical Companion." *Extrapolation (Pre-2012)*, vol. 38, no. 3, 1997, pp. 248–250. *ProQuest One Literature*.

Miéville, China. "Fiction by Reza Negarestani." *World Literature Today*, vol. 84, no. 3, 2010, pp. 12–13. *PRISMA Database; ProQuest One Literature*.

Murphy, Eoin. "Alan Wake." *The Irish Journal of Gothic and Horror Studies*, no. 8, 14 June 2010, pp. 82–83. *ProQuest One Literature; Publicly Available Content Database.*

Porter, Andrew I. "Other Obituaries." *Science Fiction Chronicle*, vol. 20, no. 6, 1999, p. 51. *ProQuest One Literature.*

Richards, John Dale, and Raymie Mckerrow. "Multiple Views of Multiple Realities: The Rhetorical and Social Construction of the Occult." *ProQuest Dissertations and Theses*, Ohio University, 2000, p. 380. *ProQuest Dissertations & Theses Global: The Humanities and Social Sciences Collection; ProQuest One Literature,* Accessed 3 Apr. 2025.

Schlobin, Roger C. "Horror Fiction: An Introduction." *Journal of the Fantastic in the Arts*, vol. 18, no. 3, 2007, pp. 416–418,436. *ProQuest One Literature.*

Stifflemire, Brett S., and Darl E. Larsen. "Physicians, Society, and the Science Fiction Genre in the Film Versions of Invasion of the Body Snatchers: Or Doctors with a Serious Pod Complex." *ProQuest Dissertations and Theses*, Brigham Young University, 2010, p. 106. *ProQuest Dissertations & Theses Global: The Humanities and Social Sciences Collection; ProQuest One Literature,* Accessed 3 Apr. 2025.

Thompson, Jeffrey Dillard, and Will Brantley. "Dark Dreamer: Dan Curtis and Television Horror, 1966–2006." *ProQuest Dissertations and Theses, Middle Tennessee State University*, 2007, p. 317. *ProQuest Dissertations & Theses Global: The Humanities and Social Sciences Collection; ProQuest One Literature*, Accessed 3 Apr. 2025.

Wood, Stephen Duane, and Ronald Bogue. ""I Could a Tale Unfold...": The Aesthetics of Horror." *ProQuest Dissertations and Theses, University of Georgia*, 1995, p. 468. *ProQuest Dissertations & Theses Global: The Humanities and Social Sciences Collection; ProQuest One Literature*, Accessed 3 Apr. 2025.

www.ingramcontent.com/pod-product-compliance
Lightning Source LLC
Chambersburg PA
CBHW071236070526
44583CB00017B/2205